Property of Chet Scott

D1679241

The BREAKING POINT

SHAWN MOSLEY

THE BREAKING POINT

ISBN #1-885342-06-3

Breaking Point Ministries
P. O. Box 4436
Muskegon Heights, Michigan 49444

Published by
Creative Ways Multimedia
509 Marie Drive
South Holland, Illinois 60473

Library of Congress Cataloging in Publication Data
Mosley, Shawn
The Breaking Point
by Shawn Mosley
ISBN 1-885342-06-3
I. Title - Original Edition
96-96280

All Scriptures are derived from the King James Version of the Bible unless otherwise indicated. Printed in the United States of America.

[illegible]
1 Cor 5:17

Foreword by

NICKY CRUZ & E. V. HILL

The BREAKING POINT

SHAWN MOSLEY

Creative Ways Multimedia

Dedication

First, this autobiography is dedicated to my beautiful wife Marie and to my precious daughter Shawndrea who were very supportive of this project. I love you both very much, my God-given sweethearts. Second, this work is dedicated to the Holy Spirit who inspired and motivated me to write my testimony. Third, this book is dedicated to Wayne Easily, a friend of mine before and after I was saved, who recently went home to be with the Lord. And last but not least, **THE BREAKING POINT** is dedicated to Robert Monago, one of my best secular friends who was recently gunned down and murdered on the streets of Florida.

Special recognition goes to David Wilkerson, Nicky Cruz, and E. V. Hill, three genuine ministers of the Gospel who have set a godly, Christlike example for me and millions of others around to world.

Special thanks must be given to Pastor John Evans, who has helped me enter into the call of God upon my life. May God continue to richly bless you.

Thanks must also be given to Al and Tracie Webb, my very special friends who undertook this project as if it were their own.

PRELUDE

In 1958, David Wilkerson's continual effort to redeem seven gang members on trial for murder in New York City was the basis for ***The Cross and the Switchblade.*** This book received immediate acclaim and became a best-selling classic and movie. David's obedience to God gave birth to one of the most outstanding evangelists the world has ever known—Nicky Cruz.

Before his confrontation with God, Nicky Cruz was the leader of the Mau Mau's, a ruthless New York City street gang. After his conversion to Christ, Nicky shared his story in the blockbuster book ***Run Baby Run.*** Like the original account, this autobiography quickly swept the nation. Twenty years ago, Nicky's testimony impacted and transformed the world.

The saga continues. The year is 1997. In gang warfare, the weapon of choice is no longer a switchblade but 9 millimeter pistols and semiautomatic machine guns. During these perilous times, there is no place to hide and nowhere to run...baby. The *only* solution is Jesus Christ! And the unanimous choice of critics and the general public is **The Breaking Point,** the best Christian autobiography of the decade!

FOREWORD BY NICKY CRUZ

The Breaking Point demonstrates the redemptive power of the cross and how the precious blood of Jesus flows to the uttermost and reaches the guttermost. This work of God gives hope to "Generation X" and puts the "X" in its proper place through salvation and the power of one man's testimony. This book will transform a prostitute into an X-prostitute, a gang member into an X-gang member, a dope head into an X-dope head, and a criminal into an X-criminal.

This story reminded me of who, what, and where I was before I accepted the Lord into my life. The misguided paths Shawn Mosley and I took were almost identical. Thank God Jesus saved us! Just as I was used by God to destroy the generational curses in the Cruz family, so Shawn was likewise instrumental in breaking the same curses in the Mosley family. Because of the life-changing power of Christ, this man of God will not continue the evil of abandoning his family or turning his back on his children. On the contrary, Shawn and his wife Marie are committed parents and up-and-coming ministers. What a wonderful testimony!

I am confident *The Breaking Point* will change whoever comes in with contact it. I strongly recommend everyone to own a copy.

EVANGELIST NICKY CRUZ
Nicky Cruz Outreach
Colorado Springs, Colorado

The contents of this book are captivating. You will be encouraged by this riveting testimony, which details the transforming power of Jesus Christ in the life of one who was enslaved to sin. The change in Shawn Mosley's person is nothing short of miraculous! Truly, God is *no* respecter of persons but rescues all who call upon His name.

REVEREND PHIL McCLAIN
Teen Challenge
Muskegon, Michigan

FOREWORD BY E. V. HILL

The Breaking Point is a divinely inspired, evangelistic tool that will impact millions in the Body of Christ and simultaneously minister to the countless people in the valley of decision who are waiting to accept Jesus Christ as their personal Lord and Savior.

This true-life account will change the way you perceive, think, feel, and treat the lost. It will spark a renewed passion in your heart for soul-winning—as it did in mine. I believe in this mission, this ministry, and this man! The world harvest is great, and Shawn Mosley is anointed by God as an end-time laborer to reach the outcast, downcast, and castaways. Every born again Christian should read *The Breaking Point* and act upon its contents to reap the masses who are blinded, lost, and destined for an eternity in hell.

DR. E. V. HILL
Mount Zion Missionary Baptist Church
Los Angeles, California

Shawn Mosley's unique writing style makes him a "diamond in the rough." It's no wonder he is emerging as one of the great Christian authors of this century! *The Breaking Point* is reaching and liberating millions who are in bondage to Satan and his evil deceptions. God is using this vehicle to open prison doors—spiritually, soulishly, and naturally—around the world.

PROPHET BILL PANKO
The Glory of God
South Holland, Illinois

Table of Contents

INTRODUCTION

As a child, I grew up without a father. Consequently, I never knew what it was like to have a positive role model in my life. Day by day, I existed under the false assumption that to be a "man" I had to project an ironclad image of toughness and emotionlessness. How wrong I was. Today, we see the devastating effects of the missing male adult in the lives of young people.

In the very beginning of humanity, it was not so. God ordained man to be the head of the woman, marriage, family, and home. As the Father of spirits, God knew the importance of a father figure. This is also the reason Jesus addressed God as "Father."

If a person has a loving and caring earthly father, it is much easier to have a covenant relationship with the Heavenly Father. God's love is much more vast and unconditional than an earthly father's love could ever be. For this reason, true disciples of Jesus must be perfected in God's-kind of love and serve with agape love.

The purpose of this book is threefold. First, to challenge the males of "Generation X" to be men of God. Second, to encourage fathers and mothers everywhere not to give up, but to trust God and fervently pray for the restoration of the family. God is on His throne and prayer changes people and situations. Third, to be a witness and weapon of reform. According to Revelation 12:11, saints overcome the devil *"by the blood of the Lamb, and by the word of their testimony...."* As my personal testimony, this book (1) will liberate countless people who are in bondage to Satan and his evil deceptions; (2) will open prison doors—spiritually, soulishly, and naturally—around the world; and (3) is guaranteed by heaven to set the captives free.

INTRODUCTION

[illegible]

[illegible]

[illegible]

[illegible]

Then it happened. Peter and Clinton began to exchange serious profanity. The argument was getting heated and hostile when Franky unexpectedly walked out of the club. Most thought he checked out. In actuality, Franky went to his car and got a 12-gauge, sawed-off shotgun. He loaded two cartridges into the barrel, hid it under his trench coat, and returned to the bar without saying a word.

Franky spoke up. "What are you hasslin' my homie for, man?"

"Butt out! This ain't between you and me," Peter said. "It's between me and Clinton. Move or you're gonna get hurt!" Then Peter roughly pushed Franky out of the way.

That was the wrong thing to do because it set Franky off. Peter became an unsuspecting victim. Before he could turn around and walk away, Peter met his doom blindsided. The sound of a single gunshot blast echoed throughout the bar. Peter was projected into the air and slammed into the wall. He fell on his chest and died instantly. His insides were splattered all over the place. Blood and flesh were everywhere.

Franky walked over, stood next to the fresh corpse, looked down, and said...

Constant Rejection

1

REJECTION IS ONE OF SATAN'S GREATEST TOOLS against humankind. It opens the door to other demonic spirits and unpleasant emotions like worthlessness, rebellion, retaliation, and hatred. Rejection is universal because the sin nature in humanity has created a divine longing and need for every man, woman, and child to be accepted.

If the devil is given the opportunity to attack people with rejection, he will damage and destroy their self-worth. This is especially true of children. It is easy for the young and impressionable to be deceived into believing they cannot achieve what other kids are excelling at. With this kind of thinking, the attitudes of inferiority and mediocrity settle into their lives. The enemy called "average" becomes a part of their person. At this point a child feels inadequate and doesn't value himself. In his heart, he believes he can never compare to others or be a successful person. This shatters the hopes and dreams of a child long before he or she realizes it. I can attest to this.

Rejection was the first thing that attacked me. It started when I was very young. I was born on May 26, 1967, in Lakeland, Florida, and was rejected by my father at a very early age. Many questions continually tormented my mind. Why was I abandoned? Why was I rejected by dad? What did *I* do wrong? How come I was different? When the other kids shared stories about the love and companionship they had with their fathers, I felt incomplete, half whole, and gypped. As they told father and son tales, I felt alone, rejected, and forgotten. I didn't even *know* my father. He had no part in my life. Therefore, to be accepted, I made up stories about an imaginary father who didn't exist.

My position in the family brought on the next form of rejection. As the middle child of seven, I was often overlooked and neglected. Demons told me I was the black sheep of the family. Not knowing any better, I believed them. With no father in the picture, my mother, Patrica Allen, delegated the responsibility of the children to my oldest sister and brother. Children caring for children. It was like the blind leading the blind. Destruction was inevitable, especially for my sister Lisa and me.

As it is with most middle children, my younger sister and brother received all the attention because they were the last ones born into the family. They were heavily favored and received special treatment. After all, they were the babies. Lisa and I were the two middle kids. The ones most often ignored and uncared-for. The devil deceived us into believing that we were unworthy of time and attention from our mother. This went on for years and years. During that period, Lisa and I received the mold of rejection that became the pattern of our lives.

When all hope for affection and attention was lost at home, I ventured to the streets to look for it. I needed to find what was not given to me by my parents. Consequently, I started socializing with people who were in the same predicament I was in—on my way to hell. To gain acceptance, I gave in to peer pressure. I began to act like them just to fit in with the crowd. They welcomed me with open arms and received me without question. I soon found myself hanging around people who felt like I did. Lonely. Disliked. Despised. Misery loves company.

As I look back on that situation, let me explain something. Satan is the father of lies. As the deceiver of humanity, he makes everything seem much worse than it is. Everything and everyone appear to be in worse shape than they really are. In reality, that's not the case. Stop a minute and look at your circumstances. Are they really *that* bad? Even if they appear hopeless, someone somewhere is worse off than you. And Satan is the worst of all! No one has been a loser longer

Mel Barth & Mike Manor

Saved out of the entertainment world, Mike's testimony and ministry is unusual and touches lives all across America ~ Don't' miss it!

Service times...
Sunday 10:45 a.m. & 6:00 p.m.
Monday - Wednesday 7:00 p.m.

Faith Baptist Church, 7729 West 48th Street, Fremont
Steven T. Tipmore, Pastor
Neil T. Wiggins, Assistant Pastor
924-2327

Special Services

at

Faith Baptist Church

May 4-7, 1997

with

Evangelists Mike Manor & Mel Barth

☆Great Music
☆Children's Program Each Service with "Marshall Mel"
☆Dynamic Preaching

than he. In essence, the devil tries to make humans feel the way he does. Forsaken. Repulsed. And everyone's adversary—including God and all of heaven.

Know this. No matter who or where you are, God is aware of your personal dilemma. The Lord's hand is not shortened that it cannot save. Neither is His ear heavy that it cannot hear. His love covers everyone of everything evil. If you sincerely ask God to forgive you—He will. Salvation is a free gift, but you have to ask. When you ask, God gives, and when God gives, you receive. However, salvation can only be received on earth when a person is alive. After death...it's too late! Don't wait. Ask God now. Today is your day of salvation. To make your decision for Christ, turn to page 149.

When I was eight years old, I met a guy named Robert who moved from Queens, New York to Lakeland, Florida. As a third grader he was extremely mature for his age. I remember Robert as being fearless. Even as a child he was not afraid of people or what they could do to him. After the first week of school, he was the most talked about, well known kid on the playground.

Before I met Robert, Jason and I were the school bullies. We were the known and recognized bad boys. When Robert came on the scene, I challenged him to prove to the other children that I was still kingpin and running the show. The playground was my turf and I was its lord. So I called Robert out. The challenge was given. I pictured the two of us exchanging blows until the best man won—me. That was one of the biggest mistakes I made as a child. Before I knew what hit me, I was down for the count. My bell had been rung and was still ringing. Robert knocked my block off.

When I was on the ground, I realized I couldn't beat him, so I joined him. This was the beginning of an ever-binding relationship that eventually turned bad. Later in our lives, this friendship was rekindled into a trio of evil called "E-Z and the Fox Partners in Crime."

I remember early in life my great-great-grandmother sitting on our front porch telling my brothers and sisters and I about her childhood. She told us that her father and mother were owned by slaveholders. Consequently, she lived most of her life in bondage to slavery. Time and again she left us with these words: "In my day, people struggled. But deep down inside, we knew a person could be anything he or she wanted to be."

I respected her and her words, which returned to me later in life. They reminded me that things didn't have to be the way they were. I could do anything I dreamed of doing.

As a baby I was stricken with a severe case of pneumonia. During my time of sickness, my 75-year-old great-great-grandmother prayed for me. She was a woman of God who was assigned by heaven to my side. The effectual, fervent prayer of this righteous saint availed *me* much! She knew how to hear from God, touch His heart, and move His hand.

One day my fever was so high that I was literally drenched with sweat. The fever caused me to lose total control of my nervous system. Even as a baby, death was knocking at my door, but neither God nor His faithful servant would let death in. Because the fever didn't break, my great-great-grandmother took me to the hospital. After the doctor examined me, he told her that I would have died a couple of minutes later.

More often than not, when a child is born into this world who is destined for greatness in God, the devil attempts to destroy him or her prematurely. It's as if Satan discerns who is called and gifted, and attacks them when they are most vulnerable.

This type of vicious assault is not new. The enemy has attacked early in life from the time of Abel. Another example is Moses. In this account, Pharaoh gave specific orders for all males two years and younger to be put to death. This was a direct strike against God's plan to free Israel. The same situation was repeated approximately three thousand years later in the life of Jesus. Satan through King Herod *tried* to destroy the Christ child at birth to abort the mission and ministry of God. With such attacks, the devil thinks, believes, and attempts to alter the plan of heaven. But no matter what Satan does, he cannot stop God. And no demon can hinder what God is doing in these last days. For whosoever and whatsoever is born of God overcomes the evil principalities of this world. Amen.

Through her consistent prayers, my great-great-grandmother and I established a godly soul tie. I became very attached to her because she mediated and snatched me from the valley of death. I was very fond of her. It was clear that she was the only one who really loved and cared for me. Or, so I believed at that time.

As a child I sensed that God was preparing me for her earthly departure. I frequently dreamed she was leaving and would never return. When this occurred, I went off by myself and wept. I asked God to take me instead of her. I honestly didn't think I could live if she wasn't around.

On May 8, 1975, God spoke to my great-grandmother and told her to take my great-great-grandmother to church. The pastor had prepared a special service that Sunday for the elderly women who had dedicated their lives to ministry and service. At church the pastor called the names of the women to be honored. Then he finally announced Mrs. Alberta Johnson.

The instant the pastor called her name, God simultaneously spoke to my heart and revealed that He was going to take her to heaven in a few days. I couldn't believe it. I didn't want to accept that God was really going to take her away from me. Before she came into my life, I was rejected by everyone and everything. She was the only one who loved me enough to intercede and nurse me back to health. If it wasn't for my great-great-grandmother, I would be dead. She assumed the position of my natural mother. She was my strength, my hope, and all I had.

I asked myself, "Why would God take away this person from my life? Did He hate me that much? First my father, now her?"

I prayed against it. When that failed, I begged God.

"Oh God, please, please, don't take the one person in the entire world who means everything to me."

Only time would tell if God heard me and answered my prayer.

My answer came sooner than I expected. Two days later when I was sleeping, I had a dream that my great-great-grandmother had died. I woke up crying. I woke my brother and told him she was dead. He looked at me and told me I was crazy. He said I had a bad dream and told me to go back to bed. I tried to sleep, but couldn't. A couple of minutes later, the front door burst open. There stood my family crying hysterically. They told me grandma was dead. My dream was true. God rejected my prayer.

I was shocked and in shock. In an instant everything inside me broke. My soul was pierced, my heart was shattered, and my faith in God was destroyed. In my devastated state, I made a vow that nothing was really important. All I had was gone. Worse yet I was all alone again. No one or nothing else mattered.

My great-great-grandmother's funeral took place on May 16, 1976. It was the saddest Saturday of my life. As my family gathered to pay their last respects, each person walked past her blue casket. When it was my turn, I couldn't move. I viewed her from my seat. From that perspective I saw an empty vessel that vaguely resembled the woman I remembered. As far as I was concerned, that wasn't my great-great-grandmother. She had gone to her new home in heaven. After several agonizing minutes that seemed like an eternity, I finally got up the nerve to approach her casket. As I gazed upon her corpse, I recalled her wisdom, firmness, and strength. Tears filled my eyes as I beheld the remains of the only person I truly loved and the only one who truly loved me.

I was hurt, confused, and very angry with God. Despite my ignorance and self-righteous attitude, God still ministered to my heart. He told me that she was gone and I had to be strong from now on. I had to continue my life until the time when I would see her again in heaven.

After my great-great-grandmother passed away, my brothers, sisters, and I were sent to live with my mother in West Palm Beach, Florida. I remember West Palm Beach as one of the most beautiful cities in the world. It was adorned with palm trees, and its shores contained an aqua blue ocean that soothed the eyes and pacified the soul. To me West Palm Beach was paradise on earth. It was my garden of Eden and a breath of fresh air compared to what I was used to.

I retained the bad attitudes I had picked up in Lakeland, Florida, and brought them into the fourth grade. It was only a short time before I beat up four kids at my new school. Fighting was necessary to reposition myself on the ladder of dominance and to climb to the top. Before I knew it, I was back in charge again. As the boss, whatever I said was law. I took anything I wanted from the other kids. Lunch money. Lunch tickets. Lunch food. You name it. Whatever I wanted, I got. When a child develops this kind of selfish attitude at a young age, rebellion is a given. That was me, to a tee! Everything was done my way or else.

I stayed at that school for only a year because my family moved to another part of West Palm Beach. My new neighborhood off 13th Street was bad—real bad. It bred guys far worse than I. These deviates whipped you first for no reason and asked questions later.

From the day I started fifth grade at this new school, I was teased. Understand something. I was not used to being teased. I was normally the instigator and troublemaker—not the victim. For the first time in my short life, the shoe was on the other foot. And it just didn't fit right or feel right.

Due to excessive financial strain, my mother couldn't afford to buy seven children the kinds of clothes other kids had. You know...the fancy kinds, the designer type. Consequently, I wore the same clothes day in and day out—all the time. Because of this, the other kids nicknamed me "Same." I despised that name. To me, it was on the same level as the worst swearword and "yo mama." More often than not, that name started a fight. I won most of the fights and only lost a few. I resorted to violence because the feelings of rejection and inferiority overwhelmed me to such an extent that I lashed back by lashing out. In all honesty, I didn't know what else to do. Fighting was the only thing I knew and did well. It kept me alive and helped me survive. The problem was that violence was becoming habitual in my life.

We lived in West Palm Beach for three years. Afterward, we

moved to Winter Haven, Florida. Like the previous moves, I took with me the debris and residue from the old hoods. The slime, grime, and crime of West Palm Beach molded me into someone I didn't like or know. The evil of the streets was becoming a part of my person. I was turning real ugly—real fast. Some of this occurred because of the destructive influences of society. However, the reason for a majority of my actions could be traced back to my home. Specifically, constant rejection and the lack of a father.

It is vitally important for parents to speak positively about their children and into the lives of their offspring. During their emotional development, children need to be continually reminded of their self-worth. Their individual vision of success must be planted and cultivated as early as possible. Once this truth is securely rooted, the devil has no basis to attack with low self-esteem. For as a child thinks in his heart, so is he. When a child knows his purpose, he will pursue it and overcome all obstacles to attain it.

While I attended school in Winter Haven, I went through the same situation. My classmates continually teased me because of what I wore and how I looked. But not all of them. There was one exception. I quickly found out her name.

Jan was tall for her age. She was a dark-skinned, attractive, young girl. Truly, beauty is in the eye of the beholder and my eyes were sparkling. We hit it off immediately, and the attraction was mutual. I could tell from the get go that I finally met someone I could be myself with. Therefore, I allowed this girl to see the real me. The inner part I hid from everyone else.

About this time my mother accepted Jesus Christ into her heart as her personal Lord and Savior. Due to her spiritual conversion, church became a weekly *must* for all of her children. I didn't mind going. In actuality, I really liked church. Not because I was religious, but because my girlfriend was a member of the same church. When the pastor preached, Jan and I sat across from one another and "made eyes" at each other. It was pure puppy love. Even though the initial reason I enjoyed church was Jan, I subconsciously learned about Jesus and His undying love.

As the years passed, Jan and I attended different schools. She went to Bartow and I went to Westwood. It didn't matter, though. Distance didn't separate us. Absence only made our hearts grow fonder.

Jan brought out the best in me—no matter what I did. For example, I was the third fastest kid at Westwood. I ran the 100 yard dash in 9.9 seconds, and Jan encouraged me every step of the way. She instilled faith in me and my God-given abilities. Jan told me I was the best runner she ever saw and I believed her. I excelled because she believed in me. When I was with Jan, I didn't feel rejected. She accepted me for who I was—clothes and all. Her approval actually unshackled me. I was free for the first time in a long while.

Then one day the dung hit the fan. Before I knew what had happened, our relationship turned sour. Jan decided she was too young to be committed. She told me she wanted to end our relationship. In my heart, I knew it was over. The first thing I did was blame myself.

"I knew it! I knew it!" I screamed. "I knew this was too good to be true."

Rejection told me I wasn't good enough for her. Then pride interrupted my pity party and said, "Who is she to dump me?"

Jan was my first real love. I respected her. I cared for her. I liked her. I loved her. Worse yet I opened up to her. She held my heart in her hands and crushed it. This was the second time in my young life that my heart was broken.

In the end, it didn't matter. I couldn't coax or convince her otherwise. She left. That day I made another vow to myself. I would never fall in love again. I was too sensitive and the pain of breaking up was too unbearable! At the age of 16, I erected a concrete wall around my heart. This kept the pain in and people out. The women of my future would pay and suffer for the hurt Jan caused me. The cycle of rejection had spun its wicked web and entangled me as its prey.

Seven years later I returned to Lakeland. Lakeland was different from West Palm Beach and Winter Haven. It was very inviting in many ways. I actually believed that Lakeland was the place where I would rise above my past failures and present hurts. It's funny how people think a geographical change will instantly erase the problems and scars that took years to create. In Lakeland I decided to experience life. Correction. The fast life—consisting of fast money, fast cars, fast women, and all-around fast living.

During the day I went to school. At night, I hung out in the clubs with the older guys. They bought me drinks and gave me marijuana. I sat around and talked with them until I could hardly walk home. The following morning, I struggled to get out of bed and dragged myself to the bus stop to go to school. Believe it or not, at the bus stop, guys who were still partying from the night before offered me a hit on a joint or a swig of beer. Rarely did I turn them down. I eagerly embraced both vices. Drugs and alcohol quickly became my means of escape.

Day after day, week after week, and month after month, I went to school as high as a skyscraper. I sat in class and either slept or daydreamed about the allure of the world and the neon lights of night. I thought about how unconditionally the world accepted me and how quickly I was adopted into its family. The streets became my new home. The scum of society replaced my immediate family and became my brothers and sisters.

It didn't take long before I lost all interest in school. My philosophy became, "It's not *what* you know, but *who* you know." The moment I formulated and accepted this thought, I was through with school. It wasn't cool. I heard about dropouts and became one.

One day after school, I went to a club called the Flamingo where I met a guy named Shannon. Every time I ran into Shannon, he had a pocket full of money and plenty of "get high." Unfortunately, I was still innocent and very ignorant. I was as green as a pool table and twice as square. Whenever I asked Shannon how he made so much money, he said things like, "I have my ways" or "I make a sting every now and then."

The lust for money gnawed at me. Whatever he did, I wanted

in—no matter what it was or how much it cost. His money-making schemes stirred my curiosity to such an extent that I got up early every morning and went to his house. I bugged him morning, noon, and night until he finally let me in on his secret. Shannon told me he regularly burglarized houses. Although I knew it was illegal, I didn't care. I begged to go on his next "job." Normally, he didn't take anyone with him, but he made an exception for me. The door to crime swung wide open. I entered at my own risk, never thinking twice or looking back. Neither did I consider the consequences of my bad decision.

The evening of our first hit, we met at eight o'clock. The plan was to go from house to house and steal valuables. Here's how it worked. Shannon rang a doorbell and waited a few minutes. Then he ran across the street and scanned the area for house watchers or neighborhood lookouts. When the coast was clear, he gave the signal and we moved in.

The first thing we did was check the windows, for most of the screens came off easily. We pushed the windows up and climbed in. If a window was locked, we wrapped a shirt around our fist and punched the window out. Once inside we had 5 to 10 minutes tops. We stole everything valuable we could get our hands on. This included anything we wanted to keep and the stuff we planned to sell for cash.

Taking things that weren't ours brought lots of money into our hands. In fact, we hit the jackpot. My conscience told me I was breaking the Eighth Commandment. A still, small voice said, "*Thou shalt not steal.*" So what! I enjoyed serving mammon. The money came in so quickly and easily that stealing became my new way of life. I thrived on the risk of getting caught and the excitement of having several pockets full of dough. I felt good about myself, for I had accomplished something. I was a self-made success who could finally afford the flashy clothes those grammar school kids teased me about. I thought I was really living high. Little did I realize, I was heading down a disastrous road controlled by Satan and the demons of hell. Truly, wide is the gate that leads to destruction, and great is the path that points to hell.

I learned a harsh reality on the street. No one cares about the people in the fast lane. Not even those who exist in this destructive lifestyle. There are two basic philosophies to life in the fast lane. First, do whatever you want. Second, get all you can while you can. The Bible offers the opposite perspective. *"For what is a man profited, if he shall gain the whole world, and lose his own soul?" and "The love of money is the root of all evil...."* Life in the fast lane is a total free-for-all. Anything and everything goes. It's survival of the fittest and the wickedest.

As time went on, Shannon and I eventually stopped "working" together. He showed me the ropes of crime and taught me all he could. The fact of the matter was I no longer needed him. So, like garbage, he was discarded in a moment's notice. Besides, Shannon started to get "hot" real fast. His name was mentioned on the streets and in the police station way too often. It was just a matter of time before he ended up in jail.

To be very honest, my heart was hardened and I didn't care. Neither did he. Shannon had his life to live and I had mine.

Down With the Boys From the Hood

2

IT WAS A WARM SPRING DAY IN APRIL, 1983, AND MY MIND was racing with anxiety and anticipation as I boarded the Greyhound bus to face a new, unexpected adventure. I was excited about what life had to offer me. After all, at that time, the world was my oyster. I went to the Job Corps in hopes of getting a new lease on life. I believed this was going to be my one-way ticket out.

As I began the ride from central Florida, my mind started to wander. I envisioned myself on graduation day receiving my diploma in carpentry. I daydreamed about going legit and making an honest living for myself. In my heart, I wanted to do right, but my mind and body had other ideas.

As the bus continued, I looked in the distance and saw the sun dancing on the freshly tarred highway. The abundance of heat waves made me appreciate the cool, air-conditioned temperature of the bus. I closed my eyes and reveled in the thoughts of my curious mind. Where was I going? What will it be like? Will there be a lot of women there? Was a store nearby where I could get a case of beer if I wanted? Before I knew it, I was fast asleep.

About two hours later I was rudely awakened by a blaring announcement. "Now entering Gainesville Job Corps!" I was forced to leave the peace and comfort of my fantasy sleep zone. Half disgusted and half excited, I wiped the haze from my eyes and reentered the land of the living. Reality was upon me in a big way. Before me was a 20 foot metal fence that enclosed a small city. The obnoxious driver blurted out for the second and last time, "Now entering Gainesville Job Corps!" Enough of that noise.

I met many new people during my first day of orientation at the center. One of the first was Charles, also known as Slick. He was a lightly complected brother with a gold front tooth and a well-polished demeanor. His nickname fit him well—for so he was. Slick was also a martial arts student. He was stocky and well built with a physique similar to Mike Tyson's. His entire attitude was money and his life revolved around acquiring it—one way or another.

The second guy I met was Lynford. The fellas called him Lil' Boobie. Lynford was from the greater Fort Lauderdale area. He was a warmhearted brother who was endowed with great influence. He could talk anybody into anything—and often did. Lil' Boobie was charismatic, very outgoing, and fun loving. However, there was a darker side to him that displayed a disturbing sense of loyalty. This side believed in any means necessary—even if it meant violence, destruction, and death.

Then there was Miami Knight. I never found out his true identity. Too many people let his Asian look fool them. This brother had his act together. He was five feet two inches tall with a medium build. The two things I remember most about Knight were his gift of gab and the mass of silver he wore around his neck. Rumor had it that Knight was so smooth he could talk his way in and out of Fort Knox. Trust me, if he had the chance, he would try. He believed in capitalizing on all golden opportunities presented to him.

Next was Ronald, or Sir Fox. This brother made a tremendous impact on my life. He was an introvert and was very clever. Ronald's whole world revolved inside his head. He was only 24 years old but possessed a lifetime of school and street smarts. He took me under his wing, imparted the realities of city life, and showed me how to conquer them. Sir Fox was levelheaded and never lost his cool. He was the very definition of calm and collected. He survived and thrived by the adage, "The hand is quicker than the eye." His hands were as fast as lightning. Sir Fox rarely resorted to violence. But when he did, it was an experience his opponent never forgot.

I quickly became his disciple. I watched him, studied his moves, evaluated his ways, and learned all I could. Without a father, I desperately longed for a role model. So I quickly derived a false sense of identity from street-smart hustlers.

The last person I met at the Job Corps was Marvin. The fellas named him Sly. Although Marvin mastered thievery, he knew next to nothing about defending himself. He was always getting dogged and clobbered by some low-life loser. Sly started many a fight that always ended with him getting knocked out. When it came to fighting, he was a total novice.

Slick, Boobie, Knight, Fox, and Sly were all hustlers. They got money any and every way possible. They gambled, tricked, stole, and sold dope. If people resisted, they threatened to lock down the flow of the almighty buck throughout the Job Corps center. These guys were the first "O.G.s," which stands for Original Gangsters. They mastered crimes I longed to first experience. Through years of trial and error, they finessed the art of street hustling.

The five hustlers and I formed an informal gang. Because I was the most naive in the group, they took me under their wings of crime. At that time, all of the heavyweight hustlers were from south Florida. This consisted of West Palm Beach, Fort Lauderdale, and Miami. Anyone not from these regions was considered an "O.B.," or Off Brand. Another derogatory name given to lightweights was "Bama." Bama was a country, back alley brother. I ranked as a big time operator because I lived in West Palm Beach and knew the slang of that city. I knew its tightest lingo and used it to fit in. I took full advantage of this opportunity when it was presented.

Slick and I became very close. We exercised together daily and practiced martial arts. Sometimes he woke me up and said, "West Palm, let's get our push-ups in!" That was the sign to work out until we reached physical exhaustion. Our bodies had to be kept in tip-top condition in case we had to fight to the finish.

In those days my life was based on threats, control, and dominance. But not everyone I came in contact with accepted my high-ranking status. On several occasions, I had to prove I could hold my own. Since my body was a perfectly tuned, well greased machine, I didn't hesitate to swing first and ask questions later. Violence was a programmed response for survival. I wanted to live, so I fought hard and won.

The New Group

3

"HEY, WEST PALM," SLICK CALLED. "LET'S GO TO the front gate, check out the fresh arrivals, and see if there's anybody new coming in from the city."

"I'll tell you what," I yelled back, "you check it out and see if you recognize anybody from the city. In the meantime and in between time, I'll check out the lil' honeys!"

"No deal, West Palm," he protested. "Why are you doin' me like that? You know I ain't laying low," he added. "Why don't both of us check out the honeys first and then see if we know any homies."

"That's a bet," I replied.

As we neared the front gate, we observed the fresh arrivals from Miami exiting the bus. There was something about the boys from the city that separated them from everybody else. They had a certain sophistication about them. The seriousness and maturity in their faces was very identifiable. They had hard core personalities because they lived in a hard core reality.

There were four new candidates from that bus for our gang. First was Lil' Dave. He was a little brother with a dark complexion and dark, curly hair. When he smiled, the sun gleamed off the two gold teeth in the front of his mouth, which were engraved like a pair of dice. Second was Jimmy Drake. Like Lil' Dave, he was a small brother with a muscular build. Although he was the comedian of the group, Jimmy Drake was not perceived as soft or weak. When push came to shove, he was as tough as they came. Third was Elmo. He was 16 years old, six feet two inches tall, weighed well over two hundred pounds, and walked with a be-bop bounce step. In his hometown, Elmo was a high-ranking member of a gang called the Dixie Players. There he was renowned for his incredible strength. First impressions last forever. I vividly remember his image when he got off the bus. He wore a V-neck T-shirt, ragged Levis, and "Chuck Taylor" sneakers. Fourth was Lil' Blue. He was a small brother, dark in complexion, who always remained very low key. Lil' Blue had no respect for anyone. No matter who or what a person was, he addressed everyone as "son." He said this in such a way that alerted everyone he was a gangster for real. And he was. His disposition was ghetto, and he interacted with everybody on that level. Lil' Blue was an unbroken brother who just didn't care. Although he was the smallest brother in the gang, he would step on the biggest toes if he had to. That was his attitude and way of life.

There is something radically different about the youth who grow up in urban America. Society whips them into shape and conforms them to its style. The geographical climate of the street matures a person by exposing him or her to the realities of life that most children in the suburbs or country never experience.

Many minorities of the inner city are forced to live in run-down apartments due to meager economics. The government designs housing projects to study the behavior of the minority. The truth of the matter is that anytime a group of people or race is under social scrutiny, they respond to their respective environment and live at limited abilities.

Welfare is another thing that keeps people in bondage to the system. Granted, everyone may need help at some time in his or her life. The key is to receive help until you can help yourself. The problem with welfare is too many people use and abuse the plan. The initial idea was a good one. Create a program for temporary financial assistance. But for the most part, welfare paralyzes people. It imprisons them with no key to escape. It's a Catch-22 situation. It is designed to limit minorities and make them dependent on the government for their financial resources rather than God and their God-given skills. Welfare restrains the potential within humanity. It confines the untapped streams of creative ability that will eventually produce success over time.

This is what happens. When a person applies for welfare, he or she is asked a series of intimidating questions. This causes embarrassment, humiliation, and further frustration. In the process, a person loses self-esteem and feels less important than the individual taking the information. The system deems the man or woman a failure who is incapable of contributing to the good of society. Welfare sends a clear message to the applicant—I am your source of money *for life*.

I have learned that every person on earth has dreams and visions of success. These include intellectual, physical, and financial success. However, most urban minorities do not believe they can obtain these kinds of success by following the so-called system. For this reason, they develop and embrace the attitude that to become "somebody," they have to step on everyone else and destroy all opposition in their path. They try to earn the benefits of success through wickedness, not goodness—by selling drugs, gambling, hustling, and participating in con games. They try every negative means possible to become a big fish in a small pond.

The concept of success is not wrong. On the contrary, God extended dominion to man prior to his creation. A majority of the time, the method used to enforce dominion is wrong, illegal, and evil.

As I watched the guys get off the bus, I relished the opportunity to turn the Job Corps upside down and inside out. The one vision that consumed my mind was to take this place over.

Within one week the first phase was in place. Our gang was formed. We were involved in everything from selling drugs to violence to prostitution. In actuality, we ran an underground Mafia. We had a form of every vice that the infamous Italian Mafia operated.

I distinctly remember one night when my gang and I went to the mess hall for dinner. Part of the daily routine consisted of complaining about how bad the food was. On this particular day, we decided not to eat the food. We waited until the mess hall was packed and began throwing plates in every direction. Within seconds, a food fight was in full-blown manifestation. Everyone joined in. People were doused and splattered with all sorts of trash.

The garbage hit the fan when a gay guy named Jay Jay went to the director and snitched on us. Because he narked, the entire crew was terminated for a whole month. As we were getting ready to leave, we saw Jay Jay walking down the hall. We approached him and asked why he squealed on us. He denied it. We called him a lying faggot and began to walk away. Just when he thought he was out of danger—wham—out of nowhere—somebody walloped Jay Jay and he hit the floor hard. It was time to retaliate. We punched, stomped, and kicked him until he was a bloody mess.

"Now run and tell, you fool" was the remark left in departing.

The Greyhound bus pulled up at the front gate on July 5, 1983. My click and I boarded and it headed south.

The 30 day release went by quickly. Before we knew it, the gang was on the bus again and back at the Job Corps center. I stayed there another month before I was permanently terminated and sent to Alachua County Juvenile Hall in Gainesville, Florida. My crime was aggravated assault with a baseball bat. The anger that raged within shattered my vision of graduation. This was the first time that I was placed in handcuffs. At that moment, I no longer felt human—more like a caged animal. Little did I know, this would be the first of many times I would feel this way. It was an indicator of worse things to come.

I tried not to cry when I was placed in the holding cell, but my emotions overruled and tears showered my face. These were long overdue tears of deep hurt and hatred.

My first taste of prison hardened my heart all the more. One thought dominated my waking mind—society would pay bitterly for locking me up. No matter what it cost, society would get what was coming to it.

It wasn't long before I formed a gang in juvenile hall. The gang consisted of country boys who were big in size but small in street sense. Because they were so dense, I didn't have to use physical reinforcement to maintain my position. I told them what to do and they obeyed. I enjoyed coaching the boys in the ways of evil.

I ran the Alachua County Juvenile Center through fear and manipulation. I had fun making those big country boys bring me weed, smokes, and booze. They actually looked up to me as if I were some kind of king. At Alachua, I rose to the very top. Anything and everything I desired was at my beckoned command.

I stayed there for only two weeks before I was sent to Ocala Detention Center. Ocala was much bigger than Gainesville. Despite its size, it wasn't long before I was back on the throne. Like Alachua, I ruled one and all with the same domineering attitude of control and power.

At Ocala, the more serious cases were sent to Mariana State School, or Doza, to serve time from three months to seven years. One memory that I will always have about the introductory stages of incarceration was disinfectant time. The chief of staff sprayed your face, torso, private parts, legs, and back to kill hair and crab lice. A 20 second stream of high pressure water usually did the trick. This sanitizing process left you raw and gasping for air. More often than not, I cussed out the person who sprayed me. Most everyone did.

During my 21 day stay in detention, I occupied my free time by lifting weights and writing letters. When the three weeks were up, I had gained several pounds and was in tip-top shape. I could do 75 to 100 push-ups at one time—no sweat! I also schemed a plan to get reenrolled in the work program. I wrote a letter of apology to the director of the Job Corps. My intention was to con him into buying my return bus ticket when I was released. It worked. He bought it hook, line, and sinker. What a sucker! There's one born every minute. The money was transferred and the bus pass was purchased in my name.

As I headed back to Lakeland, I decided to pickup where I had left off. Upon my arrival, I was reunited with my gang and resumed my position of dominance. One of the first things I did was locate my third grade buddy Robert.

Robert was very charismatic. I watched him time and again walk into a room of crowded people. One by one they ceased their conversation to listen to him. Robert was the black E. F. Hutton. When he spoke, people listened. He had more street smarts than anyone I ever met. From time to time, Robert did a small burglary to get some quick cash. But for the most part, he coerced and conned people out of their money.

I found my homie and we decided to party. Robert and I bought weed, beer, and cigarettes with the money he duped from dopes. Getting high was part of our daily routine. One day after we had finished smoking a joint, Robert looked at me.

"Hey, Fox. I've been into witchcraft for a while. I can still operate in the power. Watch!"

Robert began to move things in the bathroom without touching them. He told me he contacted the supernatural realm and a spirit named Krowbar accompanied him. Later, I discovered that Krowbar was a demonic spirit.

Instead of being frightened, I was impressed and inquisitive. I asked how I could obtain this telekinetic power. He told me one way was to fast for three days. He promised to reveal more details later. Lucky for me later never came. Every time I asked, he never told me. Looking back as a saved, Spirit-filled Christian, I know God deliberately silenced his tongue on my behalf. There is absolutely no doubt that I would have instantly and ignorantly plunged into the occult and done everything in my power to continue my reign of dominance. I thank God for sparing me the misery.

When I hung out with Robert, money always seemed to come into our hands. Despite the external success, I perceived myself getting bitter, hard, and icy on the inside. My coldheartedness was manifested as violence. For example, Robert taught me how to throw a six inch punch that could knock out a gorilla. I mastered this technique and many others. Then one night I was presented with a golden opportunity to demonstrate it.

Robert, his brother Herbert, and I were attending a street party in the park when I saw one of my arch enemies. This punk had caused me major grief in the past. I fought him over and over but could never beat the h—— out of him like I wanted to. He stood with some other people and made an unnecessary comment that ruffled my feathers. That was all I needed to initiate contact. I mounted my perfected gorilla punch and visualized the strike in my mind. Then I quietly walked over and—out of nowhere—nailed him directly on the chin. He never saw it coming. He went down like a tree and was out like a light. Mission accomplished!

I victoriously stood over him and reveled in the moment. He bled from the head and foamed at the mouth. At first glance I thought he was dead. He smacked his head pretty hard on the concrete. But I really didn't care whether he lived or died. I hated his guts. In my mind, he was better off dead. The world was a better place without him. Later, I found out he ended up with a severe concussion from that shocking encounter. I knew he would never forget me.

After that night Robert and I were unstoppable. We went into bar after bar and beat guys into a pulp. Robert was known for his ability to fight, and I learned well from my street mentor. As time went on, Robert was given the name E-Z. My street name was Fox. We palled together so much people called us "E-Z as the Fox." Before we knew it, our names were buzzing throughout the streets.

At this point in my life, it seemed like my entire existence was based on schemes. I schemed money to fulfill my fast dreams. I schemed women out of their virtues. I schemed everyone to get everything I wanted.

At that time, Phil and Maxi, two of Robert's street brothers, moved from Queens, New York, to Lakeland, Florida. The first day I met Phil, we got stoned, laughed, and talked. Neither one of us trusted the other—and we both knew it. He wanted to see where I stood, and I checked him out at the same time. We weren't about to just let anyone into our click. No way! A true candidate had to have character, heart, guts, and loyalty. To prove our worthiness, Phil and I decided to fight each other. The first time we mixed it up was when we were both high and way out of touch with reality. He was itching to attack and initiated it through a false accusation.

"Hey, Fox, I saw you checking out my girl!" Then he took a big swing at me that landed. We fought until our strength was gone and couldn't fight anymore. When it was over, he looked at me and said, "Let's go get high some more."

I quickly agreed, "Bet!"

The reefer deadened the pain and made everything a blur.

Phil was chiefly responsible for introducing me to purse snatching. We went to the mall and scouted the area for local pigs. As soon as the place was clear of cops, one of us walked up to an unsuspecting woman and asked her for a cigarette. When she removed her purse from her shoulder, it was as good as gone. Snatch and run. We always parked our car two blocks from the mall so no one could identify us, the vehicle, or the license plate number.

With the money we purchased a "blunt." A "blunt" is an empty King Edward cigar laced with a mixture of marijuana and cocaine. The blunt produces a killer buzz. It kept us high for 12 hours at a time. To me, liquor and narcotics were all there was to life.

One day a former acquaintance of mine got busted with stolen goods in his possession. The heat gave him a choice: do time or rat on his accomplices. Like a typical scumbag, he cleared himself and pimped the whole gang. Before I knew it, the police had a warrant for my arrest. I was only 17 years old and already wanted by the law. But they weren't about to catch me. Local brothers tried to warn me about the warrant, but my pride boasted they would never take me—dead or alive. When I shared the bad news with Phil, we decided it would be best to leave town for a while. Later that same night, we stole a van and headed for Miami.

When I was in the Job Corps, I had met and hung with some guys from Miami. They lived the same "easy money" life we did. Like us, they resorted to violence to remain free and stay alive. This was just another lie the devil tricked me into. I lived like a "go getter" because I was convinced that the world owed me something. And I was out to take what was mine—with a vengeance.

Phil and I cruised to Miami, which was about a four or five hour trip. Phil drove the entire way because he was the only one who had a valid license. I slept for most of the trip. Once we entered Dade County, we parked the van next to a motel and went to sleep. We were exhausted and broke.

The following day the glorious morning sun woke us up. Miami is such a beautiful city. Its palm trees, trade winds, tropical climate, and summer scenery remind me of another world—namely, heaven. Despite its natural beauty, Miami is also known for its smugglers, drug lords, and heartless violence. In Miami, all is fair in the name of war. And only the fittest and the biggest guns survive.

That morning we drove around the city and admired its scenery. We were temporarily free from the fear of being fugitives.

After a couple of days Phil started missing his babe and decided he wanted to go back to Lakeland. I seriously considered the idea. The more I thought about it, the more I agreed to return. Besides, neither one of us knew how to care for ourselves in a big city like Miami. But we had a dilemma. We didn't have the gas money to return home. Therefore, we drove to the local mall with the intention of robbing someone. We cruised around for about 10 minutes and lay low until we noticed a woman coming out of a bank. Phil and I had to move fast. We parked the van instantly and got out.

I slowly walked toward her and smiled as if to say "hello." She smiled back. The moment I passed her, I turned around and grabbed her purse. At first she wouldn't let go. I figured she couldn't hang on forever and I wasn't about to give in, so I dragged her along the street. She finally released it, and I left her screaming in an alley. The purse and all of its contents were mine.

I quickly crossed the street and noticed a police car up the road. An overweight security guard was standing at the entrance to the mall. I discreetly tucked the purse under my arm before I passed by and smiled at him. The stupid blimp was none the wiser. He smiled back, and I continued on my merry way. I was scot-free. Yes!

When I got to the van, I looked around to make sure no one was following me. The coast was clear. I got in and ducked down. All of a sudden, I heard someone whistling as if to get my attention. I peeked up to see who it was. To my surprise it was Phil. He jumped in the van and we bolted. The sting produced $300, which was split 50/50. We headed back to Lakeland busting up the entire time about the expression on the lady's face we just robbed.

The first thing we did upon arriving in Lakeland was to purchase a blunt. Phil gave me the money and cocaine to hold while I ran for brew. On my way back, a raucous caught my eye. I looked across the street and saw the police hauling Phil away in a squad car. I quickly fled that scene. My first thought was, "Poor Phil." Then a second thought crossed my mind, "Better him than me." Now I'd just have to get high by myself. It was a good thing that I held the money and coke. After all, I really didn't care what happened to Phil. In the street, everyone is expendable.

The heat was on and I needed cover, so I went to a friend's crib to hide out. Along the way I ran into a guy named Frank. Frank was a complex dude. He was the kind of brother who would give you the shirt off his back if he knew and liked you. But never double-cross him. No one wanted to get on his bad side. Frank lived by the gun, and others died by his gun. When he had to use it, he went all out. He hadn't lost a gunfight to date.

Since Phil had gone to jail and was locked up, I asked Frank and his lady if they wanted to get high. An emphatic "yes" was all I needed to light up and we left. Getting high by yourself is a drag. Drugs love company. The three of us got zonked until all of the drugs were consumed.

I thought best stoned. It was a very familiar state of mind. I decided the time had come to move to another location. As I tipped out of the Lakeridge Projects, I looked across the street and saw that a large crowd had gathered. Everybody was standing around talking about something. As I got closer, I overheard a conversation between Curvin and his brother Shawn.

"I thought he was dead."

"Yeah, man. I walked over to him and he wasn't even breathing."

"I wonder who poisoned him?" they asked.

Then Shawn looked up and said, "Hey, Fox! They found your boy laid out in the park. Somebody slipped a mickey in his drink and poisoned him."

"My man...who?" I asked.

"Robert. They just rushed him to the hospital," he answered.

"Is he all right?" I urgently demanded.

"I don't know. It looked pretty serious."

I got myself together and immediately left for Lakeland General. As I entered the hospital, I saw Robert lying on a bed with an IV sticking out of his right arm. He was accompanied by his mother. The two of them were talking and laughing together. I breathed a major sigh of relief. As soon as we made eye contact, Robert's countenance brightened. He was very glad to see me and I him. It's a shame that more unity and brotherly love exists among heathens than believers. For saints—not sinners—are admonished to greet each sincerely and affectionately.

In the streets we learned to depend on each other for guidance and support. Many people in the streets have a giving spirit. I have met bag people who didn't own a thing but would give you their last penny. This kind of dying-to-yourself attitude is desperately needed in the Body of Christ. Those who freely give of their own will prosper. For God blesses the cheerful giver.

I talked with Robert until the wee hours of the morning. Only then was everything still and quiet. No one roamed the streets. The city had finally settled down and a temporary peace blanketed the area.

My personal tranquillity was interrupted by the thought of the pending warrants against me. I hated the fact that I was wanted by Johnny Law. Besides, the pressure and anxiety of getting caught was almost maddening. What should I do? Turn myself in? If I did, maybe they would just slap my hands and give me probation.

Early the next morning I looked around for some of my buddies. I hoped to find someone...anyone to change my mind. But no one could be found. I followed through on my initial plan and headed for the police station to turn myself in to the authorities. I figured they would acknowledge my good deed and go easy on me. Wrong! Unfortunately, the thought of probation never entered their minds. Instead, they held me for three hours until an officer came to my cell and transferred me to detention in Bartow.

The following week at Bartow I caught up with Phil, and we resumed our old tricks and bad habits. We ordered around the other inmates just as we did during our days on the streets. Most obeyed, some rebelled. I had to fight day in and day out to maintain my position of authority. From time to time, I overheard the other inmates say, "Look at Fox, he's one crazy dude. Don't nobody mess with him."

"You got that right!" I mumbled under my breath.

I stayed in detention for three months. Afterward, I was released to a halfway house in Orlando. During this period, I had plenty of time to scheme and dream of more deviate ways to be successful.

I left the halfway house four months later. While I was there, I manipulated a man into giving me a job. I worked hard and saved approximately $500. The first thing I did upon my release was visit The Chinese Wig Shop. I bought two thick silver neck chains. One had a medallion of an African princess and the other the head of King Tut.

I was already planning my reestablishment into society once I hit Lakeland. I desperately desired a new direction and wanted a clean identity. In May of 1984, I boarded the bus that headed for Lakeland with renewed expectations. Along the way, my good intentions were interrupted by evil desires. I constantly meditated on how I was going to overthrow the neighborhood. My heart and mind were in a definite power struggle. My one aim was to be boss, for dominion was in my blood.

On the bus I stole a pound of marijuana from the girl I sat next to. My hand was quicker than her eye. When the bus reached Lakeland, I got off and searched for my old friends. The first thing I did was hail a taxi. The young guy who drove the cab looked pretty hip, so I asked him if he wanted to get high. He did. I bartered dope for a ride. The agreement was to take me anywhere I wanted to go in exchange for a joint. He agreed. We drove around for hours in search of a familiar face but came up empty. The entire night was a complete waste, so I went home to rest. Tomorrow was another day. I might as well slow down and take it easy.

Home was my uncle's house. When I arrived, I was surprised and taken back that he was happy to see me. He wanted to catch up on current events, but I wasn't in the mood to talk. I had other things on my mind, namely, a pillow and 40 winks. I explained how exhausted I was and eased my way into the bedroom. I lay in bed thinking about how good it felt to be free from the halfway house. What a relief!

I stared at the ceiling in the comfort of my bed. I fantasized and strategized how to move in and lock down the city. I was excited about regaining the respect of my peers and those who didn't know me. Within the depths of my heart, I knew I was going to be the center of attention. I loved that!

The next day was absolutely beautiful. Lots of sun and warmth. I was awakened very early by the harmonious chirping of a flock of mocking birds. I got up, strung my jewelry, headed for the door, and hit the street.

Several hours passed. Then I came across a familiar face. The first person I met was Maxi. He was very happy to see me. We reminisced about old times, and he asked where I had been. I lied and told him I had been visiting some relatives in Miami. I spoke up.

"Maxi, from now on we're goin' all out. The stake is no longer about petty cash. No sir! We're goin' for the gusto," I said soberly, not cracking a smile. If a nigga is gonna do time, he might as well go all out and not go down faking." He agreed.

I quickly adopted this lie as my new motto. Another demonic deception. With this new license on crime, I became more involved in grand theft auto and armed robbery. But my main "M.O.," or Mode of Operation, was burglary. Burglary was the vice that ushered me into the big leagues of crime.

For example, one hot summer day, a guy named Melvin and I were hanging out, drinking Colt 45s, and smoking blunts when our money ran low. Since we didn't want our buzz to end, we mapped out a local apartment complex and decided to do a "B. & E.," or Breaking and Entering. Melvin and I were so out of touch with reality that we broke into apartment after apartment and took valuables in broad daylight. In a matter of minutes, we had enough things to sell for cash to continue our high. The stolen goods were stashed in the back of a car we heisted from an old man in the building. When the time came to move the goods and cash in, the damned car wouldn't start. We tried again and again, but it just wouldn't turn over. Neither one of us was thinking very clearly because we were too doped up. Worse yet the car was parked only two buildings away from the last apartment we hit.

Then, out of nowhere, the place was crawling with bacon. Twelve police cars pulled up and surrounded us. A very dirty dozen. Apparently, one of the tenants we robbed came home and called the cops.

As the police approached the stalled vehicle, I told Melvin to stay cool. "No matter what happens, don't panic."

I sobered up quickly because I knew we were in big trouble. The lump in my throat grew bigger, and the knot in my stomach got tighter. I tried to look as innocent as I could, but I couldn't fake it because I was so stoned. The police cars got closer and closer until they were upon us.

One officer stopped his vehicle next to mine, rolled down his window, and addressed me. "Are you boys having car trouble?"

"No!" I quickly said. He continued to question me.

"What do you have in the back seat? Do you mind if we run a quick check on your license plate?"

"Man...why do you crackers always harass me? Because I'm black? I'm gonna get your name and badge number and report you for discrimination!" I yelled. It was a poor attempt to throw him off that failed miserably.

"Make sure you write my badge number down correctly because there were several apartments that were broken into today and you're going to jail."

We were busted with the hot goods on us.

"Get out of the car slowly and put your hands in the air where we can see them."

This time I was on my way to the big house. The days of small time were over. There would be no more detention centers. I just purchased my first one-way ticket to the slammer.

I was abruptly escorted to the county jail and placed in a holding cell that reeked of urine. The three hours I was there seemed like an eternity. Afterward, I was taken to the Bartow County Jail, which had an even more repulsive smell of urine. The stench was so vile I almost vomited. Within the center of this holding cell was a drain that was used as a toilet when the real john was occupied. The cell was approximately four feet by six feet with one door and one opaque window above it.

I remained a prisoner of that rot pot for seven hours. At midnight the guards came in, relieved me of that stench pad, and took me to my permanent cell. I was quickly and roughly escorted up an elevator to the second floor. Cell 22A was my home for an unknown period of time. There was a minimum of eight men to a cell—minimum. As soon as I stepped inside, that all-too-familiar fear and anxiety clutched me like a vise grip. Just as before, I knew I had to prove myself if I was going to remain alive. I did so without hesitation.

For the first two days I didn't say a word to anybody. During this time I realized that silence has a great mystery to it. I meditated on how to defend myself if someone tried to cross me. Attack was only one means of survival. If confronted, I would go all out to kill him—and die in the process if it was necessary.

After a couple of unthreatening days, I lightened up and got to know some of the fellas. I met Kenny, his cousin Kujo, Benny D, and Deon. Of the four, Kenny made the greatest impression. He was an old con, about 45 years of age, although he looked more like 35. Kenny had been doing time since he was 15 in places like the Florida State Pen, the O Unit, Sumter, and the East Unit. After serving three decades in the big joints, Kenny walked out of each without a scar.

Kenny had a muscular build and was known as the "house man"

of the cell. His ability to "slang and bang" earned him a don't-mess-with-me reputation. No one in their right mind came up against him. Others who did learned the hard way. For this reason the inmates gave Kenny a great deal of respect. Most of it was faked, but he received it anyway—especially to his face. Kenny's person and presence transformed other inmates into "yes men."

His cousin Kujo from Detroit had the rep of a young fool. Rumor had it that he regularly got involved in shoot outs and high-speed chases with the cops. Kujo was 35 years old, had a very quick temper, and an itchy trigger finger. Both Kenny and his cousin took to me because they perceived that I was a young man with guts and spunk. I displayed an "ironclad" image on the outside on all occasions.

I told them from the get go that I wasn't afraid of anyone or anything. The truth was that a desire to survive existed on the inside. The bottom line was I wanted to live. On more than one occasion, Kenny looked out for me because we were "homies." We speculated about the future and shared about the past. We planned what we were gonna do once we "turfed" again.

One time I told him about a robbery I had committed, and this startled look came upon his face. He was hurt and angry—to say the least.

He looked at me square in the face and said with a fatherly voice that restrained tears, "Fox...listen up, man. This life is for losers. Stop the cycle while you can and are still ahead. Forget the dumb stuff. Enjoy your life. You've got so much living to do yet. When your time is over, get out, go straight, and live right."

It was as if God Himself momentarily spoke through Kenny and warned me about the future. The next instant his disposition changed, and he was back to his hard usual self. I never forgot the look on his face or the words he said.

Benny D and Deon were the other two guys I met in the cell. They were in for armed robbery and attempted murder. Evidently, they robbed a gas station under the influence of crack and beat the owner until he almost died. They were sentenced to 21 years and sent to prison to fulfill the term.

Benny D and Deon were from Lakeland. They had high hopes, dreamed of playing in the N.B.A., and had the talent to match. One day the five of us were in the yard when Benny D and Deon were hoopin' against Kenny and Kujo. Benny D and Deon were running them like Ex-Lax—inside out. It wasn't long before the whippin' became a total embarrassment. It was such a trounce that Kenny got mad and swung at Benny D. Before we knew what was happening, everybody was fighting. It was a barnyard brawl. The four of them pounded each other for at least 30 minutes before the corrections officer stepped in and finally broke them up.

Later, when we returned to the cell, I asked Kenny why he started the fight.

"We made a bet on the game and were losing so bad I fought to bring the game to a forfeit."

"Why didn't you just pay them the money?" I asked.

"I didn't have it. And I don't like to owe anyone anything."

Two days after the fight, Kenny was released from jail. The cell was very different after he was discharged. Our father figure was gone. Even though Kenny was a gangster, he had a genuine side to him. I discerned a part of him that hurt for young men. Guys like me who were destroying their lives before they got started.

Before Kenny left, he occasionally confided in me. He told me he was too far gone for help. Yet he didn't want the younger brothers to make the same mistakes he did. Kenny didn't realize that with God *no one* is too far gone! Do you remember the thief on the cross? God only needs a minute and a repentant heart to give you a new start.

I woke up early the following Monday morning and found myself in the same damp, cramped jail cell. Like I was really going somewhere. It had been a long, exhausting weekend. We smoked weed and played cards the entire time. I still felt the numbing effects of the drugs. I decided to check out the local news. When I did, I received the shock of my life. The headline story in the *Lakeland Ledger* described a black man who was shot to death on Fifth and Kettles. A drug deal went sour, turned ugly, and resulted in fatality. The reporter identified the victim as Kenny Williams—the same man who was just released from my cell. I was blown away! So was Kenny. He was killed only three days after receiving full freedom. What a waste! Kenny had a good heart but his ways did him in. I couldn't help but wonder where he was spending eternity.

I spent six months in the county jail before I was sentenced to three years in prison. Then one morning around three o'clock, the correctional officer came to my cell.

"Mosley, pack your bags. You're going to Lake Butler."

I got up, brushed my teeth, washed my face, and rolled up the mattress. I had finally learned my lesson. Or, so I thought. I was ready to do my time, get it over with, and get on with my life. I wasn't about to end up like Kenny.

Before the bus left, the prisoners were fed "shangles" which are biscuits smothered in sausage and brown gravy. Then all the transferees were placed in a small holding cell called the cage. The cage was only eight feet long by eight feet wide. We piled in and waited for our names to be called. Once a person's name was called, he was handcuffed and shackled. After a prisoner has been secured with iron chains, he can hardly walk. You talk about physical imprisonment. This was it! Afterward, the captives were placed in a van that headed for Lake Butler.

As the journey began, I looked out the window and watched the sun rise. With wide-open, expecting eyes I admired the natural beauty of the outdoors. It had been over six months since my eyes beheld Mother Nature.

As the van drove through the business district of Lakeland, I saw my old buddy Frank riding his bike to work. He had finally wised up, left the crime world, slowed his life down, and held a steady job as a garbage man. I thought about how lucky he was to be free. I envied his liberty. Franky eventually disappeared from sight. I watched some of my old hangout spots zip past. Memorial Boulevard, S & B's, and the Jamaican Club. Ah...the good old days. I quickly closed my eyes and reminisced. Then I forced myself to put Lakeland out of my mind. I had to make a serious mental shift to prepare myself for prison life. I was going to be there for at least a year. I wasn't worried though. During my stay in the county jail, I had improved my fighting ability and had built up a few new muscles.

I stayed awake the whole trip. I knew this experience was going to harden me all the more. I expected jail to make me as tough as nails. I wasn't disappointed. The bus finally entered Lake Butler County around noon. In the distance, through the haze and heat waves of midday, I could see the prison. It looked like an ancient, walled castle with a huge gun tower stationed at every corner. As the bus got closer, I looked up the three story towers and saw many guards armed with semiautomatic weapons. When the van pulled into the gate, I noticed at least 12 representatives from other counties releasing their prisoners. Broward, Dade, Duval, Hillsborough, Orange, Palm Beach, and Seminole, just to name a few. Each van carried at least 10 men per vehicle.

As soon as our county group stepped off the van, we were approached by an attending guard who said, "In Lake Butler all convicts are niggers to us! We want you to know that in advance." Thanks for the warning.

Lake Butler was more like a boot camp than a prison. All cons were sent here prior to their permanent placement. Lake Butler was designed to break prisoners. The results of this temporary testing place determined a prisoner's final destination. For example, a broken con was sent to a minimum security prison; an unbroken con was sent to maximum security.

Over the years, I heard a lot about this place. Rumor had it that the guards took justice into their own hands and killed the inmates at will. For this reason, I wasn't about to say or do anything stupid. I took great pride in my ability to play people—especially the "C.O.s," or Commanding Officers. On the outside I smiled, complied, and went along with the program. But on the inside I cursed them to death, hell, and beyond! All of the C.O.s were rednecks. With every breath, their damned southern drawls got on my and everyone else's nerves. Their hick dialect actually provoked inmates to fight. The C.O.s hated city boys and had a jar full of gold teeth to prove it.

It was time to check in. The guard escorted us down a long hallway and made the men strip down. They hosed us with lice spray, sent us to the showers, and assigned prison blues. I was given the number 104853 and was taken to the "L" wing. This wing was prepared for first-time offenders who had shorter sentences because they committed less serious crimes. The wing consisted of two-men cells that were designed for the safety of the youths.

I stayed in the "L" wing for two weeks before being sent to Lancaster. There I hooked up with some of my old street homies, namely EE, Darryl B, Kee-Kee, Lil' Jeff, and T-Whiskey. We were glad to see each other. We hung out, drank, and reminisced about our past lives on the outside. A week later I was sent to Hillsborough Correctional Facility.

Hillsborough was more laid back than the other prisons. To pass the time, I got a job on the outside and worked throughout the city of Tampa. For the first six months, things were going well—very well. Then my violent nature resurged. I got involved in a major prison riot that led to a charge of assault. I was promptly sent to the county jail and stayed there for one month before all charges were dropped.

Hillsborough no longer wanted me, so I was transferred to Sumter. Sumter had the reputation of the worst youth offender camp in the state. It was known for its riots, rapes, murders, and ongoing violence.

Many of the deviates at Sumter were strong candidates for my new gang. The first was a guy named Shorty who was incarcerated for shooting a store clerk during a robbery. Next was Lil' Adidas. This brother actually shot someone over a pair of gym shoes. Can you believe that? What an idiot! Both Shorty and Lil' Adidas were considered "B.G.s," or Baby Gangsters. Although they were under 18 years of age, they received mandatory sentences of 25 to 50 years. Then I met Ringo Bid. He was from Boyetteon Beach and was as strong as an ox with hands to match. This brother would grab guys around the neck and lift them off the ground. At such a time, his victims were in the hateful hands of fate. The last person I met was Big Law. He was from Bel Glade, which is just outside of West Palm Beach. He stood six feet seven inches tall and was as solid as a rock. There was not an inch of fat on his entire frame. Although he regularly bench pressed 540 pounds, Big Law never got into any fights. He was too strung out on steroids and from weight lifting.

In prison, a person receives respect on the inside by the offense he committed on the outside. The harder the crime, the more respect. The weaker the crime, the less respect. This rule is true unless the crime was deviant in nature like raping a helpless woman or violating an innocent child. In prison, Satan gives honor and respect to those he used the most to hurt and destroy humanity.

I got settled in, took my rightful position, and became part of *their* click. It felt strange not to be calling the shots or running the show. This was the first time that *I* was the small fish in the big pond. This occurred because Shorty, Lil' Adidas, Ringo Bid, and Big Law were street warriors who had a lot more experience than I.

A certain area at Sumter reminded me of Sodom and Gomorrah. In this division, homosexual activity and all manner of perverse debauchery continued around the clock. Most of the participants were gay before being jailed, but some weaker men were forced into it against their will. At first, it was a sad and vile situation to witness. But after a while, the shock ceased because I numbed myself to it. As grotesque and repulsive as homosexuality is, it is an undeniable part of prison life. When you think about it, homosexuality is lust in reverse. I thank God I was never forced into that kind of situation because I would have killed the pervert and been sentenced to life for murder.

At Sumter, a guy named K-D hooked up with another brother who was known as Dixon. The two sold drugs, stole cigarettes, and other things. When K-D first arrived, he was broke. Dixon lent him money and cigarettes to help him out. Financially, K-D wasn't too sharp upstairs. He gambled away all of his money. In debt, desperate, and out of his mind, K-D broke into Dixon's locker and stole everything valuable. He thought no one was looking, but someone was watching. K-D was caught red-handed in the act. A guy named JR was the only witness to the double-crossing. Word quickly got back to Dixon.

"Yo, Dixon! Today while you were in class, K-D broke into your house and stole your stuff."

Dixon couldn't believe his ears. He hung his head, walked away, and didn't utter a word. Then the bell rang, which was the signal to return to the dorm. Dixon waited for K-D to get situated before he began the act.

He asked the whole dorm, one by one, "Hey, man, did you break into my house?"

Dixon saved K-D for last. When he finally asked, before K-D could answer, Dixon busted him in the mouth with the butt of a combination lock. As soon as the metal struck flesh, blood exploded from his lip like a broken water vein. Everyone in attendance turned his back as if nothing was happening. We all anticipated that the grim reaper would take K-D away. Sumter Prison was cold like that.

Dixon beat K-D until he was unconscious. The prison C.O.s were eventually called and carried him out. We all thought K-D was dead. Later, it was discovered that he survived and was sent to another prison. The truth of the matter was that Dixon had to make an example of K-D. Failure to retaliate or act in a manner contrary to revenge would have destroyed Dixon's reputation. The rules had to be followed. Theft was not tolerated, and betrayal was punishable by death. K-D was lucky. In some prisons every move a person makes is a gamble with his life. Sometimes you don't know whether you're going to make it from one day to the next. Your existence and future are in the hands of the Highest Power.

I finally finished my time at Sumter. In my mind it seemed like an eternity. In reality, I was back on the street 18 months later.

The Pimp Game Ain't Dead

4

WHEN I GOT OFF THAT OLD FAMILIAR BUS IN December of 1986, I was back in Lakeland. It seemed like I just couldn't get away from this place. Maybe destiny played a part in it. Who knows? Regardless, it felt really good to be free. What a relief! Little did I know my freedom was going to be very short lived. Because of good behavior, I got out of jail early with a year of probation pending. If it were up to me, I wouldn't do one more day of time.

Once I turfed, the first thing I did was look for my home boys. None of them could be found anywhere. I heard through the grapevine that all of them were in jail doing time. With no one to hang out with, I returned to my uncle's house until I found a lady to live with.

The next day I was awakened by the telephone. It was Bid, one of my crime partners from years past. He had just gotten his release from the army.

"Hey, Shawn, what's up?" he asked.

"Hey, what's up, homie?" I then asked.

"I have some important news to tell you. Man, I'm ready to do it."

"Do what?" I asked.

"Don't you remember our conversation when we were just B.G.s? We agreed that when we got older we were gonna pimp ho's," he continued.

"Oh, yeah! That…I remember, nigga. Pimps are born, not made," I continued. "What's the deal with the military scene you've been giggin' on?" I asked.

"Man...I just got out of the army. Now I'm gonna fulfill *my* dreams—not Uncle Sam's. Are you with me or not?" he asked.

"Okay, nigga. I'm with you," I responded.

"Listen, Shawn. I've got to go back to North Carolina for a week to sign some papers and finish packing. Can you track down a ho' to make the run with me? I'm long overdue for some female company."

"Of course. No problem!" I told him.

Although I said "yes" with my mouth, I knew in my mind and heart that I told a bold-faced lie. But I gave my word, and Bid was counting on me. So I decided to give it my best shot and just make it happen.

My first prospect was a young girl named Dawn, who was 18 years old and very well developed. She didn't have much happening between her ears, but what matters with pimping is what's on the outside—not the inside. Dawn was one of those girls who tried to be too mature for her age. I picked up on this and used this strategy to persuade her. I approached her cautiously.

"Hey, Dawn. What's up, cutie?"

"Nothin' much."

"Can I buy you a drink?"

"Absolutely! I'd love one."

It's been said that the way to a man is through his stomach. Experience has taught me the way to a woman is through a drink and flattery. I bought her one drink, then another, then another, then another. This babe could drink like a fish.

The first thing I focused on was how mature she was. I instilled the lie that she was beautiful and every man's dream. How incredibly fortunate I was to be in the presence of such a jewel! I said anything and everything to coerce her. I went for her heart and could tell by her reactions that it was working. After a couple of hours of this hypnotic manipulation, I asked her to take a trip with me to North Carolina. She agreed to go. I prepared for the trip and called Bid to inform him of my success. The "ho'" was willing to travel with us. My task was complete.

I told Dawn we would come by her house around midnight, pick her up, and head out. When we arrived at the time of our scheduled rendezvous, she was nowhere to be found. I was pissed. The stupid tramp stood me up. Nobody dis'es Mosley and gets away with it. It was a good thing that Dawn blew me off because I was going to pimp her brains out. She would have been sore for an entire month. It really didn't matter though. I assured Bid that we would find some ho's in Fayetteville and put them to work.

As we exited Florida and crossed the Georgia state line, a rush of relief hit me. It was so refreshing to finally be out of the sunshine state. For the first time in my life, I was about to fulfill my dreams at the expense of someone else.

The drive was a very long haul. We arrived in Fayetteville about 15 hours later. My first impression of North Carolina was not a good one. As we cruised the city limits, we saw the remains of the marketplace where Negro slaves were sold many years ago. Fayetteville reminded me of one thing—bondage. And I hated prison with a passion!

During my temporary stay, I witnessed crack-fiend pimps physically beating their prostitutes for drug money. These ho's were forced to trick so the pimps could buy a quick fix and continue their habits. This scene depressed me to no end. These niggers were poor, lost hustlers who did whatever it took to maintain their high. Although I was repulsed by this way of life, Bid was impressed by this abusive lifestyle. This was not unusual. Most everything impressed Bid because he was as green as a pool table and twice as square. He had no street sense whatsoever. Worse yet he had a weak spot for women. This brother had his work cut out for him.

That evening we went to a nightclub and met a couple of women who played a serious beat game. Their plan was to find a weak brother and con him out of his money. The first lady was called Cookie and the other Sandra. Both of them were very good looking with shapes to match.

As soon as Bid scoped out these hustlers, he looked me straight in the eye and said, "That's our trap! Let's lay, play, and pimp."

Even though I agreed, I didn't think Bid could hold his own. These women were way too slick for him. I tried to tell him so, but he wouldn't listen. He thought he knew what he was doing. I wasn't about to argue with him since he had all the money.

During my various stays in prison, I talked with numerous pimps and learned how the game was played. Pimping is based on mental psychology and mind control. It imprisons a woman's mind and causes her to do anything—and I mean anything—to gain and keep the affection of her pimp. Pimping preys on both male and female emotions. It sugarcoats lust as counterfeit love. It is diabolically deceptive and demonic in nature. The Bible admonishes saints to submit their bodies unto God as a living sacrifice that is holy and acceptable to Him.

I met one pimp named Fat Jimmy who gave me three basic rules: (1) never respect a ho'; (2) never let a ho' see your weaknesses; and (3) never tell a ho' you love her. This was the basic understanding of pimping in the streets.

This mentality and negative perception of women came easy to me because I had been so hurt in the past. Since I didn't love myself, I wasn't about to love anybody else—especially a woman after the way I had been devastated. No way...never again...it was pay back time!

Bid was the complete opposite. He fell head over heels for any woman and every woman. He respected every lady he dated and always displayed his weaknesses. What a fool! I had a lot to teach him, but Rome wasn't built in a day. Molding Bid was going to take time, lots of time. The ho's he partied with that night did exactly what I expected. Cookie and Sandra conned Bid out of his money. All of it. He bought them beer, weed, cocaine, and anything else they wanted. Bid was really beginning to cramp my style. Deep down inside I was pissed off because he blew our dough on bimbos. In reality, I didn't care about Bid or anyone else. I was all alone in this big world.

Two days before Christmas, Bid received a check from the army for $2,000. This time, I was going to control this action. I wasn't about to let the ho's take it, so I kept him away from women and the streets. We also needed to save money to return home. Bid was itching to travel and asked me where I wanted to go for Christmas, Florida or D.C.? Florida was old hat. Besides, I wanted to see the action of the big city. I had never been to the capital, so we hit the highway and headed for Washington.

As soon as we reached the outskirts of the metropolis, I knew D.C. was my kind of city. We drove through the ghetto and saw pimps styling new Caddies, jumping their prostitutes for cash, and collecting money at every corner. These brothers did well—very well. They dressed in Louis Vuitton suits and wore Gucci watches. This scene really impressed me because in prison I was told that pimping died in 1975. Here it was December 1986, and the pimp game was alive and booming. Despite its success, it needed a couple of new players. I told Bid to check out these brothers to see how it was done. We stayed in D.C. and studied the pimp game intensely because we were dedicated to it.

On the second day of our stay, we left our possessions in the car and walked into the city. We paid a homeless guy to watch our vehicle and gave him a shot of gin as a bonus. The more I thought about this bum watching our goods, the more paranoid I became. I envisioned him breaking a window and stealing our stuff. Therefore, I ran back to the car and found him standing alert with our stuff intact. Because he was honest, I gave him another tip and swig of spirit.

We spent the entire day touring the city. When it got late, we called it a night. It was too late to drive back to Florida, especially since Bid and I exceeded the legal drinking limit. I suggested getting a hotel for the night. Bid adamantly refused because he didn't want to spend any more money. This infuriated me to no end. He wasted a lot of money on women and all sorts of vices but wouldn't cough up 20 lousy bucks so we could get a decent night's sleep. Give me a break!

"What do you intend to do then?" I asked. "Pull out the sleeping bags and crash in the car?"

My sarcasm didn't phase him. He actually thought it was a good idea. I was so mad it took every last ounce of self-control not to fly off the handle, rob Bid, and beat him to a pulp. Lucky for him my conscience intervened. It reminded me that I grew up with Bid and considered him my homie.

At that moment, as far as I was concerned, Bid was better off in the army. The life of a hustler just wasn't his scene. I grabbed a sleeping bag and prepared to meet the sandman. Unbeknown to me, Bid drove in front of the White House. Of all the places to park, Bid had to choose the president's residence. We called it a night, eager to put the day behind us.

I fell asleep very quickly and thought I was having a nightmare. Around 3:00 a.m., we were rudely awakened by flashlights and drawn guns. The D.C. Metro police had surrounded our vehicle and spoke to us over a raspy bullhorn.

"Raise your hands where we can see them. Don't make any sudden moves or we'll blow your heads off!" They were dead serious.

I was enraged to the core. I wiped the sleep from my eyes and looked at Bid. I wanted to punch him out so bad I was shaking, but I refrained because I had to deal with the cops. The police inspected us, the vehicle, and our possessions as if we were foreign spies. I was surprised they didn't strip search us. Thank God we were clean! They let us go but wanted to impound the car because Bid's license plate had expired. I wanted to escape this situation more than ever. For once in my life, I hadn't done anything wrong. After repeated conversations, the police agreed to release our vehicle if we called a tow truck. When the truck arrived, we paid the driver extra cash not to tow the car into the pound. He agreed. *Money* almost always works. Instead, he parked our vehicle in a vacant lot. We stole a set of legal plates from another car and got back on the highway. It was 5:30 a.m. So much for a good night's rest.

The drive from Washington, D.C., to Florida was just under 18 hours. When I was back on my home turf in Lakeland, everyone I met told me the police were looking for me because I violated my probation. Deep down inside, I hated being wanted by the law. In great stupidity, I paid no attention to their warnings because as far as I was concerned, I wasn't going back to the slammer.

It was early, around 9:00 p.m., so Bid and I decided to check out a few nightclubs on the strip. S & B's was the first place we stopped. Most of my peers hung out inside and sold dope outside. Even though S & B's was classified as a hole in the wall, it was normally packed to capacity with all types of lowly street life. I was attracted and attached to the night scene because it made me feel like a star. In my own little world, my street reputation made me famous. Being a big shot temporarily filled the void of rejection in my life.

The Bible says that sinners love darkness rather than light because their deeds are evil. Before I got saved, I personified this verse. I never thought about anything good. I idolized drugs, fornication, illicit gain, and revenge.

Upon entering the dimly lit nightclub, I scanned the room and observed a man arguing with a woman. Troy loudly accused Madonna of cheating on him. The estranged woman nailed him below the belt by stating that if he were a real man she wouldn't need to look anywhere else. It was obvious that she didn't respect him. She bolted out the back door, and he exited the front. I seized this opportunity and made my move. Without a moment's hesitation, I chased after her. I repeatedly yelled for her to wait, but she walked even faster. I finally caught up with Madonna and grabbed her by the arm.

"Didn't you hear me call you?" I asked angrily.

"I don't even know who you are. Let go of my arm and get out of my face!" she demanded.

"I ain't lettin' go until you hear what I've got to say. I know you think you're bad. That's cool. I don't have a problem with that. But, you need to realize I'm the baddest and if I call, you come running and see what I want. Is that understood? The problem with you pretty girls is you think you're God's gift to men," I told her.

"Okay...now will you let go of my arm?" she asked.

Before I released my prisoner, I looked behind her and saw a mud puddle. I pushed her into it and walked away. She was so upset, she swore at me profusely. The only way to deal with street women is to be firm. Otherwise, I would be considered a pushover. There was no way my pride would allow that.

Two days later I crossed paths with Madonna at the Jamaican Club. I tested my prowess and called her over. This time, as soon as I caught her attention, she dropped everything and came over to find out what I wanted. With that single encounter, I broke her and stole her self-esteem. Because of her natural beauty, Madonna was used to men bowing and catering to her every whim. She quickly realized she was number two on the streets because I was number one. I took great pride in that type of dominance.

Within one week's time, I had Madonna conning men out of their money to buy me nice outfits. I temporarily shacked up with her because the police still had a warrant to arrest me for parole violation. Therefore, her crib became my hiding place. During my stay she bought me everything I wanted—marijuana, beer, and gold chains—even if it meant spending her welfare check. Although I quickly earned Madonna's respect and she treated me well, I didn't give a crap about her. Life was all about me. I was a selfish, egotistical pig.

Then one particular evening my luck turned sour. I decided to spend the night at my uncle's house because Madonna started to get on my nerves. She was getting too attached, and I didn't want that to happen. What I didn't know was that the local sheriff's department had staked out my uncle's house to apprehend me and take me to jail.

As soon as I was inside, I retired to the extra bedroom and opened the window to get some fresh air. The cool breeze relaxed and refreshed me. I fantasized about the fast life and dozed off.

Early the next morning I was awakened by a knock at the front door. I jumped to my feet, ran to the door, and looked through the peek hole. To my alarm, it was the Polk County Sheriff's Department. Oh no...the law had found me. In an instant, I ran back to the bedroom and dove through the open window. As soon as I tucked and rolled, I was face to face with a growling police dog and two 9 millimeter guns pointed at me. There was no question about it. I was headed back to the joint.

Down the Same Old Dirty Road

5

THE OUTLOOK THAT DAY WAS AS CLEAR AS GLASS. But I was headed down the same old dirty road. During the first week of my trip, I stayed at the Polk County Jail. Afterward, I was sent to the stockade for three months to await further sentencing. I couldn't believe it. I had been out of jail only 21 days before I was back in the same situation. It seemed like prison had its sharp claws in me and wasn't about to let go.

The stockade had a different atmosphere than I was used to. It was much more laid back than I expected. Believe it or not, to this day the stockade has a special place in my heart. This pen was the place where I was introduced to the Bible and actually read it for peace. One day, I just happened to turn to Acts 12 and read about Peter being thrown into prison. This account reports how the newfound Church prayed until an angel appeared and unshackled him. I believed this was a sign from heaven that I was not going back to prison. I speculated on the possibility of God doing something supernatural like releasing me from bondage, and letting me go back on probation. Therefore, I prayed a selfish, religious prayer hoping that God would hear it, honor it, and give me another chance. This was wishful thinking on my part. Unfortunately, it didn't work. I went back to prison anyway.

On the road to the big house, my first stop was Lake Butler and then to New River West Unit for continued processing. My new identification number was A-104853. The letter "A" indicated that I was a second-time offender.

While I was detained in prison, I was assigned to a counselor who tried to figure out what made me tick. He was thoroughly impressed with my natural and street intelligence. Many times after the end of a session, he shook his head and said, "What a waste of smarts."

I read a lot of different books to pass the time in prison. I especially liked the biographies of gangsters and hustlers like *Wise Guy* by Henry Hill. These factual stories revealed the inner workings of the Mafia and how it used violence to gain power, prestige, and most important—money! These thugs had the guts to die for what they believed in. I really enjoyed these books because my mind was always in the gutter. (Truly, the carnal mind is the enemy of God.) I wanted to know and thoroughly understand the mentality of my kind. I was hooked and deeply immersed in the street life.

I left New River and was sent back to Sumter for two weeks. After this I was assigned to Sumter Forestry Camp, which was directly adjacent to the main compound. When I arrived at the facility, it seemed like God finally had mercy on me and answered my prayer. Sumter Forestry Camp was a virtual picnic in comparison to the other prisons I had stayed in. And there weren't any gun towers either!

The daily workload was light and very refreshing. Every day we ventured into the state parks to chase, catch, and feed horses. On occasion we were allowed to swim in the lake. Serving time at Sumter Forestry Camp was a breeze. It was almost as if we were free. A single park ranger was our only guard. This guy had eyes in the back of his head. He didn't care what the prisoners did as long as they pretended to hide it from him. I greatly looked forward to driving out that gate, going into town, and visiting the parks.

One afternoon our group was assigned to repair a fence that ran into the middle of a deep swamp. As soon as we got in the water, we crossed paths with a water moccasin. Two other guys unknowingly treaded past the serpent. As soon as I saw it, I stopped and realized I was inches away from an eight foot, poisonous snake! Worse yet it was coiled and in position to strike—me. I was gripped and paralyzed with fear. I intensely stared at it, and it gazed at me with shallow, evil eyes. Then, all of a sudden, I heard a sound of movement behind me. I saw the flash of an ax out of the corner of my eye. The next thing I knew, I heard the slicing sound of sharp metal tearing into live flesh. I looked up and saw the snake cut in two, wildly writhing in the bloody water. Five minutes later I was still standing in the same position in shock and dripping with sweat. My life flashed before my eyes in an instant. Despite the manual intervention, I didn't stop to think that if it weren't for God protecting me, I would have been bitten and probably died.

During my stay at the forestry camp, I met two brothers from Miami. The older was nicknamed Tip Cat and the younger was named Lea. Even though Tip Cat came from a family of dope dealers, that wasn't his bag. He was renowned as a "jackboy," or a person who robs dope dealers. I was told that Tip Cat went to drops and robbed the whole gang, stealing both drugs and money.

Tip Cat was in the process of finishing up a three year mandatory sentence. He only had six months left to do, was trying to stay clean, and couldn't wait to get out. From time to time we talked about perfecting our hustle once we reentered reality. At that time, quitting the street game was the last thing on our minds.

One day Tip Cat and I were working outside the gates when an "O.G." from way down south confronted us. This bum had the nerve to tell us to our faces what he planned on doing to us. Even though we had almost completed our time, Tip Cat and I weren't about to stand for that crap. No nigga was gonna dis' us even if it meant more prison time. Respect has its price. If push came to shove, we would break him down and do him in. Tip Cat and I discussed the situation and came up with a plan. Our scheme was to throw a handful of sand in his face and then beat him with an ax handle. One more uncalled for remark to either of us would initiate the strategy and his own destruction. Fortunately for him, the "O.G." never said another word to or about us. He made a very good decision. It was also fortunate for us because such an attack would have postponed our parole. He must have gotten wind of our reputation and plan, and straightened up.

Tip Cat's younger brother Lea was a boxer at heart. The first time I met him was in the gym. I watched Lea pound one and all who climbed in the ring. Even though he whipped every challenger that stepped toe to toe, I didn't think Lea was so bad. Besides, all of this fighting made me want a piece of him myself. So I decided to put on the gloves and teach him a lesson or two. I knew a lot about street fighting, but "anything goes" doesn't apply in the gym. Boxing was a completely different animal. Lea and I waged war for three rounds. By the time the match was over, he knocked me down three times. Lea got my respect the hard way—he earned it.

Lea let me work out with him and trained me as a boxer. Lea told me he liked me not due to my fighting abilities but because I didn't fear God or man. I learned to box quickly because I had a knack for the sport. After a while, it became second nature and an addiction. Boxing was like a drug. Every minute of every day, I looked forward to my next opportunity to slug it out with the best of them. I took fighting very seriously and trained harder for it than anything else I had done in my life.

Lea, Tip Cat, and I stuck together. If a problem existed or arose, we went all out to solve it. Then fate broke up our union. One day when I came in from my work detail, the dorm guard told me to get my belongings and meet him at the front gate. The work release center had accepted me. Yes! I was so excited. My mind raced with anticipation. I quickly got my stuff together and rushed toward the entrance. I was headed back to Lakeland. For a long moment my heart went out to Tip Cat and Lea. There was no time to say good-bye. All I could leave them was a pair of pajamas someone had given me and a pair of house shoes. After that, I never looked back. I didn't have to. I was headed for new territory.

In November of 1987, I was again sent to Lakeland. Four hours later I returned to the work release center. I stayed there for three days before I was sent to Bartow Work Release Center in Florida, to partake in a special "Tap" program. At that time, I had only 21 days left on my prison sentence. Despite the freedom on the horizon, I had a big problem. I couldn't get a job because every prisoner was required to stay at the center a minimum of 30 days before applying for work.

While I was at the Bartow work release center, I met many

women via the telephone. During many of the conversations, I manipulated them into sending me money and cigarettes. I made them promises that I had no intention of keeping. I told almost every female I spoke with how much I loved her and that we were meant to be together. I lied to them the entire time, and they believed me. The truth of the matter was I wasn't about to settle down with anyone—no matter who she was! I was living too fast to slow down, and I intended to stay that way.

To pass the time in the dorm, a few brothers and I played cards and gambled. You know...nickel/dime ante. One day you won, the next day you lost. Although it was never verbalized, everyone internally planned his future the moment he hit the street. If a brother decided to return to the "old life style" he couldn't go halfway. He had to go all out or get out of the game completely.

Over time I began to understand the legalities of the prison system. I realized that someone who commits an occasional crime *can receive the* same amount of time as someone who is a repeat offender. In the eyes of the law, a crime is a crime. All violations are illegal and all violators are wrong. When it comes to the judicial system, no one gets a break.

During my spare time (and I had a lot of it), I read every book I could find on the "gangster" life. Two of my favorites were *The Mack* and *Ice Burg Slim.* Through these literary works, I overloaded my mind with corruption. These books and others served as the foundation of my thoughts, words, and actions.

I made many drug connections when I was in the work release program. I figured if I made the contacts now, I wouldn't have to look for them when I got out. This would allow me to make easier drug runs in the future. And speaking of drugs, I continually fantasized about wasting a few big drug lords and taking over their territories. I meditated on murder daily. I envisioned myself mustering up the guts to pull the trigger. BANG! In my mind it was a done deal. I just needed the occasion to do it in the natural. After all, this was the lifestyle I wanted and chose.

At this point in my existence, human life was inconsequential—including my own. Men were better off out of my way or dead. And women were either whores or harlots. They had a choice. Give me money or keep walking. I had evolved into a demented, narcissistic wretch. I dreamed of being a successful hustler and wasn't about to let anyone or anything stand in my way.

Makin' It Happen

THAT PARTICULAR MORNING, THE SUN SHONE VERY brightly. I fulfilled my sentence and was out of the prison system with no probation or community service wrap hanging over my head. Once again, it felt good to be free.

When I was released from the Bartow work program, two administrators gave me $100 to get a new lease on life. But like a typical fool and the prodigal son, I squandered the money on riotous living. I went to the Jamaican Club, slammed many brews, and bought a pound of weed. The right thing for me to have done was to find a job. But instead, I believed the lie that no one would hire an X-con or repeat offender.

I bought some plastic bags, divided my weed into quarter ounces, and decided to resell it. I went to the local hangouts and told the drug dealers I had a limited supply of fine Gonja weed. It sold quickly and I doubled my money. This continued for two weeks until Madonna came back in the picture. Evidently, she had looked all over town for me since the day of my release. Word on the street was that she was on the prowl. I was also on the move and didn't want to check her out. Nor did I want to be entangled in a bad relationship. I was on the run again. This time, in a different way.

6

When Madonna finally caught up with me, she came correct. She gave me $200 and invited me to go on a shopping spree. In her eyes, I needed a new wardrobe. I wasn't about to disagree. Sometimes I had to hustle all day just to make $200. And here she was handing it to me on a silver platter. Not to mention the added bonus of upgrading my wardrobe and getting a piece on the side. I couldn't pass up this deal, so I went for it. I had nothing to lose and everything to gain. I wasn't about to bite the hand that was feeding me.

Madonna and I talked about old times. We laughed about our first meeting when I pushed her into the mud puddle. All of a sudden in the midst of our reminiscing, a seriousness gripped my heart and reality set in. In the past, Madonna worked as my con artist. But as a pimp, I needed a whore, not a con artist. She was going to do what I wanted—like it or not.

Then Madonna ruined the moment and evening. She broke the news to me gently. While I was in prison, she met and got involved with another guy. He was madly in love with her and would do anything she asked. Despite his obvious affections, Madonna claimed he was too weak for her. She needed someone strong.

"Does the nigga have any money?" I asked her.

"No," she replied.

"Then drop him like a bad habit. You don't need some broke brother hanging around sponging off you."

She explained that he was a family man who wanted to settle down and have children.

I looked at Madonna dead in the eye and said, "What? You're the stupidest ho' in the world if you think you can settle down and be a housewife. You ain't nothing but a con artist and that's all you'll ever be! Stop tripping, sister!"

Madonna was shattered. That instant, her self-esteem hit rock bottom and she reached her **BREAKING POINT**. Her fragmented state was prime time to capitalize on my dream. During this absolute low period, Madonna would do anything I demanded. I told her that I didn't want her dropping me just because she got herself another sugar daddy. That night she left Ray-Jay.

The next day Madonna got an apartment and we shacked up together. I was so consumed with pimping that I could hardly sleep. The idea haunted me in the night season. Many times, I woke up thinking about it. Then one night, I acted on my dream. I woke Madonna up, took her to the street, and beat her until she was willing to sell her body. I took out a lot of my anger and hatred toward women on Madonna. Even though Ray-Jay was a softy, I knew she was better off with him than me. But it was too late for that now. Or was it? Madonna sold herself once before she dumped me and went back to Ray-Jay. To maintain my street composure after she left, I told some of the brothers, "A ho' ain't here to stay, a ho' is here to pay!"

With no ho' under my thumb, I sold weed as a side hustle. I want to relate a truth about pimping and street life. It can be very dangerous and self-destructive to do a woman wrong. They have no loyalty whatsoever. They'll betray you in a second and then set you up to be killed. When a man "dogs" a woman and destroys her self-worth, she will retaliate...sometime...someway...someday. Count on it.

Two days after Madonna left, she came back. She told me she wanted us to get back together. Like a fool, I believed her. One night Madonna invited me to her house and I accepted. I never noticed it before that night, but her house had only one door. That meant there was only one way in and one way out. As soon as I got settled in and comfortable, someone kicked the door in. There stood Ray-Jay and his friend Cedrick with wooden clubs. It was a trap. I was set-up. That b——! They came in and Madonna ran out.

They beat me with their clubs. The first blow was to my head. I remember feeling the warm blood ooze down the side of my face. Then my vision doubled and got blurry. I thank God I never lost consciousness. Who knows what would have happened to me.

They continued to swing away and I fought back. I didn't fight to win, but to survive. I fought to stay alive and was wearing down fast. I felt life's energy draining from my body. In my dazed condition, I schemed one last strategy. (It's amazing what the mind will think of to stay alive.) I pretended to fall unconscious. I hoped they would slack up enough and give me an opening of escape between them. They did. That was all I needed. I shot through their legs, staggered out of the apartment, and ran for my life. But where? To my uncle's house.

As soon as I was inside, the first thing I did was find something to nurse my wounds. Once I was bandaged up, I frantically searched for a weapon of destruction. I hoped for a gun, but only found a hammer. It would do. I grabbed it and headed back to Madonna's place. I envisioned taking the claw of the hammer and smashing their skulls with it.

Now it was my turn. I returned to the apartment and kicked the door in. The place was empty. I searched the streets, but they were nowhere to be found. Lucky for them, because I was going to kill them on the spot. I got tired of looking and was completely exhausted, so I went home to sleep and recover.

The next day I got up early and went to Robert's house. I knew he would help me quench the vengeance that raged within me. I told him what happened and he responded appropriately.

"Let's get these fools!"

"Do you have a pistol?" I asked.

"Yeah...but I ain't goin' down with no 187 murder charge!" he said.

I could have pressed him to change his mind, but I was in such a hurry I didn't push the issue. I wanted revenge and I wanted it now! I found a shovel, cut the handle off, and wrapped it in electrical tape.

The first place we checked was the pool hall. I peeked through the back door and saw Madonna and Cedrick. Jackpot! Two out of three. Not bad for starters. I told Robert to station himself at the front door. When both entrances were covered, I initiated the sting. I slammed the door open and caught everyone by surprise. Cedrick looked up, saw me, and bolted for the front door. Robert entered and stopped Cedrick in his tracks.

"Hey, fool! Where you goin'? What's up with you bangin' on my homie?" Robert poked Cedrick in the chest with the end of the handle. "Back up, nigga. You ain't runnin' nowhere!"

Cedrick walked backward into the center of the pool hall. I moved in position, dropped my weapon, and laid a straight right jab that nailed him in the mouth. Robert was about to pounce on this fool when I stopped him.

"No, he's all mine, man. I want him all to myself. I want his blood on me."

I didn't want to use the shovel handle because that would have been too fast. I wanted him to experience slow pain and suffer at my hand. So I beat him until I was tired and he was unconscious.

Like a typical ho', Madonna didn't run, but stayed to watch the thrashing. When I was done with Cedrick, I seized Madonna. I had to teach her a lesson. No one double-crossed me. I beat her with a closed fist until blood repeatedly spurted from her mouth. Then I grabbed her by the hair, dragged her across the floor, and kicked her several times in the gut. When I left, she was crying hysterically and curled up in a ball. Two down—one to go. Ray-Jay was next. Robert and I spent the rest of the day looking for our last victim. Evidently, someone got word to him, he checked out, and was incognito.

I continued to sell drugs. I saved my money and bought an ounce of cocaine. I added substitutes to the compound and started selling it as crack.

One day while at home, I received a telephone call from Bid. At first I was disgusted. But on second thought, it was good to hear from him.

"Hey, Shawn, what's up?" he asked.

"Same old, same old. What's up with you, baby boy?" I responded.

"Yo, I know the last time we worked together I was a little square," he told me.

"More like a Rubix Cube," I said jokingly. "But what's up anyway?" I asked.

"Things are different now. It's goin' on and I'm stacking a lot of paper. I'm pimping ho's, slamming Cadillac doors, and putting punks in my trunk."

I responded out of ignorance. "You're full of s——! Nigga, you ain't got it like that. You might as well get your head out of the clouds, come back to earth, and quit living in fantasy land."

"Man...I tell you what. Since you don't believe me, why don't you come down here and check me out for yourself?" he offered.

"That's a great idea. Count me in," I said.

I packed my bags and was off on another road trip. Bid lived in Alburndale, Florida. For a small, hick town, a lot of money floated around Alburndale. When my feet hit the ground, the first thing I did was walk down a little dirt road named Hobbs Lane. As I moseyed down the beaten path, I noticed crack fiends everywhere. I looked across the field and saw another major street. As far as my eyes could see, women of all colors stood on street corners looking for a sucker to trick so they could buy some cocaine. After an hour of checking out the hood, I saw a familiar brother walking toward me.

His first words were, "Nigga, look around and behold this major operation. I'm the big money man in this town. All of this is mine!"

I responded in amazement. "Bid, you weren't pullin' the wool over my eyes, were you? You're really living large, nigga. Way to go, bro'!" I said.

"Yo, Fox. My name is no longer Bid. Everybody around here knows me as LC." LC it was.

I bought $300 worth of crack from LC and started selling it. I made myself a promise to never use crack because I witnessed the devastating effects it had on people. Over time, it takes control of a person's mind and body. People do crazy stuff for crack. Mothers forsake their babies and men forget their responsibilities—all for a hit of this lab drug. Crack is a very jealous drug. It will not share an addict with another drug. Crack will consume you until it totally possesses you. Once possession has taken place, death is right around the corner. This occurs because a high-ranking demonic principality is attached to this drug. No one is strong enough to fight and overcome crack without the delivering power of God.

Before long, LC and I were running most of the city. I had six ho's working for me and LC had the same. We pimped with crack for money. Here's how it worked. First, we gave the ho's free crack to get them hooked. After they were hooked, they sold their bodies for us in exchange for a continual supply of crack. Once they were caught in the addiction cycle, there was no way out. We had them ball and chain. So did Satan.

With an abundance of cocaine around, I decided to try it. I figured one time couldn't hurt. When I did, I liked it. So I tried it again and again until powder cocaine owned me too! Most of the time my life consisted of staying out all night, riding around, drinking beer, and snorting coke.

The crack fiends brought me all kinds of jewelry, VCRs, video cameras, guns, and clothes. They offered me anything and everything of value just to keep their supply of "medicine" coming.

Selling drugs and pimping women gave me a sense of power. I thoroughly enjoyed the dominion I exercised over others. I had finally fulfilled my dreams. I was the big fish in a small pond. However, in the process, I became colder and harder by the day. For example, I beat dope fiends down for $20 and pushed prostitutes out of my car as I rode down the street. Despite my evil temperament and manifestations, addicts and ho's faithfully returned to their master—me. I really went off the deep end when I exalted myself as a god and demanded that the entire city bow to me. The Bible commands humans to worship the Lord God—no one else.

There was only one drug dealer in the city who had more power, influence, and drugs than I did. His name was J-Rod. At 17, he had the reputation of a young fool with a happy trigger finger. J-Rod was known for drive-by shootings. He fired first and asked questions later. If someone owed him money, instead of a smile, he greeted them with a 9 millimeter or a pistol whipping. From time to time, J-Rod gave me drugs to sell for him, but I never paid him back. I looked for an excuse to rob, shoot, kill him, and take over his turf. When he confronted me about it, I told J-Rod straight out that I wasn't going to pay him. He respected my nerve and humbled himself before me. He too was weak.

One day, one of my ho's named Karen gave her earnings to another local pimp. This infuriated me beyond belief. When I saw Karen I grabbed her by the throat and choked her until she passed out. I left her for dead in the middle of the street. Later, I heard that she survived.

Occasionally, when I came down from my drug trips, I took a short break from life and analyzed myself. I couldn't believe how I was acting. The more I examined myself, the more I disliked the monster I had become. I had evolved into the personification of hatred and evil. Because I couldn't handle the truth and didn't want to change my lifestyle, I consumed coke around the clock to escape reality. I contemplated suicide but dismissed the idea because it was too easy a way out of life. If I was gonna die, I didn't want to die alone. Someone else would have to kill me. In the process, I would take three or four others with me.

Every so often I pondered my childhood and the way my great-grandmother raised me. Because violence wasn't in the picture, I couldn't figure out what happened to me. Where did I go wrong? The real question was, "Where didn't I go wrong?" One thing was certain. Even though I drank and used drugs to drown the pain, I couldn't escape my own conscience. And although I thought I was on my way to the top, I was sinking quickly. I was young and very stupid.

I had witnessed the consequences of people who acted violently. He who lives by the bullet dies by the bullet. I was so arrogant that I actually thought I could go through life mistreating people and get away with it. How wrong I was. A man reaps what he sows. Unfortunately, I had sown too many poisonous seeds. I was sure the law of eventuality would catch up with me and come back to haunt me. It was only a matter of time.

You Reap What You Sow

AT THIS STAGE IN MY LIFE, I LIVED ANYWAY I WANTED to. No one cared. And no one tried to stop me. I was strictly out for self-gain and self-gratification. My world was on the verge of extinction. God wasn't going to let me continue to hurt people without experiencing their pain. It's funny how humans think they can go through life unaffected by the bad decisions they make. Most exist as though they own their lives and don't owe anyone an explanation for their actions. This was my outlook on life.

I have come to realize that two opposing beings affect and control this world. These are the regenerate power of God and the degenerate power of Satan. If a human being is not led by God, he or she will be directed by Satan. It's either one or the other. Although I possessed a great deal of power and influence over people, I still wanted more. The lust for power is one of the ultimate deceptions of the devil. For it was the root of his own fall and destruction.

One morning around one o'clock, I decided to retire from my frills for the evening. I went to a local hotel and picked up a woman to spend the night with. She was very attractive and had just started to use cocaine. While she prepared her line, I snorted my coke. Her excessive fidgeting caused me to look up at her. I noticed she was very nervous and shaking from head to toe.

"What's wrong?" I asked her. What she revealed greatly intrigued me.

7

"I have a boyfriend who introduced me to witchcraft," she said. "He would have sex with me without physically touching my body. I know the occult is wrong and I tried to leave him many times, but he has a power over me that is so strong I cannot leave. I feel like

I'm his prisoner."

The instant I heard about this power, I wanted it. I developed an immediate craving for it. I recalled Robert demonstrating his power to move objects without touching them. I concluded this was the same type of thing. I put two and two together and realized this power was obtained through witchcraft. I continued to press her until she told me about *The Book of Shadows.*

I had to have it, so I asked her, "Do you know where your boyfriend keeps his black book of witchcraft?"

"Yes, I know exactly where it is."

"Can you get it for me?" I asked.

"He never lets me near it. But if you give him some crack, he might let you use it for a while."

I wanted to make a good first impression, so I gave him a large amount of crack. It worked. He allowed me to borrow his book.

Let me reveal something to you. With drugs, the addiction *always* gets worse and the craving is *always* for more. My first addiction was alcohol. This was followed by marijuana. Then it was weed laced with cocaine. After this, my addiction progressed to straight coke. Then it was crack. When it got to this stage, I did something I promised myself I would never do. I got high on my own supply. All the time.

As I read Satan's counterfeit of the Bible, I heard an audible voice speak to me. The voice knew my name. It spoke clearly and to the point. "Shawn, you can use crack and not become addicted!"

Many months later I realized that audible voice was the evil one attempting to keep me bound to drugs. The devil is a liar.

Although I had witnessed the destructive power of drugs firsthand, with this book in my possession, I felt invincible. I could actually feel a supernatural force surging in my hands. (Later, I discovered this power was demonic in nature.) I truly believed that with the aid of this book, I had the power to use and abuse drugs and still hold my life, mind, and body together. How wrong I was. This was just another evil deception. Satan gives no one such protection—not even the children of hell. I double-damned myself by reading the first chapter of the book and snorting crack at the same time. This continued all night until I ran out of drugs. I smoked over $300 worth of crack that night. When I finished early the next morning, the owner of the book came by and picked it up.

The Bible warns humans not to be ignorant of Satan's schemes. I was not only ignorant, but downright idiotic when it came to the devil's devices.

That day I was so wired that I couldn't sleep. I spent the rest of my waking hours searching the floor inch by inch for a speck of the white stuff. I did this because I had a "terrible jones." A "terrible jones" is the stupefied state when a person's mind is continually calling for more drugs and his body constantly craves it. It's a terrible predicament to be in because a person will do anything for another fix. The "terrible jones" overrules common sense and the conscience that says "no." It says "yes" and acts accordingly to keep the high going.

I looked for more crack until I passed out on the floor. When I awoke a half-day later, the pleasure of the high lingered in my mind. I wanted it again—no matter what the cost. A part of me was concerned about becoming a junkie, but another part didn't care. It only wanted to experience the high again.

Satan keeps people in bondage through memory recall. He reminds them of the good feelings they experienced during the act of sinning. Take sex for instance. Sex itself is not wrong. God created sex to be a pleasurable experience between a man and a woman only in marriage. The devil perverts this pleasure and uses the "good feeling" to lure people into premarital sex, extramarital affairs, and homosexual activity. These vices lead to all sorts of problems that eventually result in the destruction of the body and even death. It's the exact same thing with drugs. If the devil can get a person hooked on the "good feeling" of a high, he'll influence that person to do it again and again. This also leads to any number of problems, including stupors, overdoses, and comas. Truly, the wages of sin are death.

The devil knows what feels good and uses the bait of sin to entrap and destroy billions of people. The problem with Satan's temptations are twofold. First, they are carnal pleasures. Second, they don't last. This is why it seems you can never get enough of a deceitful pleasure.

Eternal pleasure exists only in heaven. And only in God's presence is the fullness of joy. The great thing about God's-kind of high is that it's absolutely free. It doesn't cost a believer anything. God's high will liberate a saint—not imprison him. And he can maintain the buzz of the Spirit as long as he wants to. The irony about God's-kind of high is that it's the real thing! Alcohol, drugs, sex, money, and other worldly pleasures are all demonic counterfeits. I wish I knew then what I know now. But unfortunately, I didn't. I almost perished because of a lack of knowledge.

After that experience, I stayed clean for two months. This continued until one day when I gave in to the temptation and that old familiar feeling. The draw consumed me until I caved in.

Bid and I spent the whole night together and drank a fifth of gin. After Bid passed out, I checked him into a local hotel and made sure he was comfortable. Then I stole an ounce of crack and the $200 he had on his person. I decided to leave Alburndale and headed back to Lakeland. My steps were ordered by the devil, for I drove straight to a crack house. I spent the rest of that night and the entire next day smoking crack. About 11:00 o'clock that evening, I felt extremely nauseous. I began to perspire profusely as sharp pains shot through my chest without warning. My heart raced faster and faster as adrenaline was pumped throughout my system.

I visualized my heart bursting open when I heard a voice in my mind say, "You're gonna die. It's all over for you."

Then I remembered I had $160 and three rocks of crack on me. I knew if I passed out, the other dope heads would rob me and dispose of my body. An alarm went off inside me that produced an instinct to survive. I stood to my feet and started for the door. One of the dope fiends saw me and asked, "Hey, Fox! What's up? Where ya goin', man?"

He didn't care about me. His only concern was that I had the drugs. I didn't tell anyone what was happening, and they were none the wiser. I was too afraid they would kill me if they knew how weak I was. I said nothing and continued for the door. My heart felt like it was going to explode. It pounded harder and harder and harder. That instant I remembered my mother telling me that there is power in the name of Jesus. I finally got to the door, turned the handle, and thrust myself outside.

In great desperation I called out, "Jesus! **Jesus! JESUS!**"

I stumbled across the street to an elderly man's house. I asked him to call an ambulance. The pain was so excruciating that I thought I had suffered a severe heart attack. The ambulance took its time. When it finally arrived, the paramedics analyzed me and confirmed that I had indeed suffered a heart attack due to excessive drug use. I couldn't believe it. The devil tried to destroy me, but Jesus saved me. I personally experienced the reality of the Scripture, *"Whosoever shall call on the name of the Lord shall be delivered...."* I did and was. Because I acted on this verse, I was saved from death and an eternity in hell.

You would think that after experiencing a life and death crisis, I would wise up and come to my senses. Nope. Not me! I was too hardheaded, hardhearted, and full of pride. I was also enslaved to a demonic spirit of addiction, for I had developed a drug habit of $1,000 a day.

I vividly remember walking the dark, lonely streets of the city in the middle of winter with a severely drug-induced mind. I was completely deranged and quickly became a threat to everybody's safety. I was a menace to society and a danger to everything good. I conned anyone who possessed the means to supply my addiction. For example, I remember when I was at the local liquor store, I met this big, white brother who was looking for marijuana. I asked him if he was in the market for weed, and he said "yes." I told him to meet me in the alley behind the store. I went out back, looked around, and found an empty cigarette package. I removed the cellophane and stuffed it full of *natural* grass. I approached the dude and told him we needed to move fast because I didn't do slow transactions. He grabbed the package and inspected the bogus goods.

"Hey, man, this ain't weed," he protested.

As soon as he spoke those words, I hit him square in the chin with a right hook. It struck pay dirt and he was out cold. After he settled on the ground, I stole his money and headed straight for the crack house. It was time to get high.

I lived for my "high" 10 minutes at a time—day in and day out. Crack gives a person a feeling of euphoria. You fly sky-high, but when it's over you crash real low. Crack leaves a person very depressed and with a strong yearning for more. It uses you, abuses you, and then tries to kill you.

Crack became my master. I worshiped it well. That drug demanded and received my undivided attention. I gave it my heart, mind, soul, body, and life. I lived for this drug and did everything to get it. It became such a constant dependency that I desired crack more than life itself. That's how bad I was hooked. I tried to withdraw from the addiction of crack, but it was much stronger than my will. Try as I did, I could not break free from the drive or the desire. Consequently, I gave in and adapted to the crack lifestyle.

When I smoked, I resorted to my evil ways. I robbed houses again and committed three to five burglaries a day. I also stole from department stores. To break into houses, I punched out windows with my bare hands. Blood ran from my cut flesh like water, but I was so drugged up I didn't feel the pain. This type of insane activity continued for six months. I did whatever it took to satisfy my insatiable craving for that drug. Throughout the term of my addiction, I stole over $100,000 worth of merchandise to support my drug habit. As if this weren't bad enough, my life took a detour for the worse. In time I became a derelict and a street bum. In broad daylight I broke into houses. At night I slept in abandoned buildings. I stole everything I could get my greedy hands on. Despite all of this sin, deep down inside, a faint voice cried out to God for salvation. Little did I know the worst was yet to come.

A few weeks later I visited my mother. For some reason, when I was at her house she insisted that I kneel and pray. Maybe she discerned the trouble I was in. In retrospect, she was led by the Spirit of God. Even though I didn't know God personally, I prayed anyway. Afterward, I went about my business and resumed my unlawful activities.

One week later to the day, I did something that brought me to the brink of death. I broke into a certain house and stole everything of value. This included a set of sterling silver and some precious jewelry. This was one house I wished I had passed on. I hocked the goods to different drug dealers but held on to a few things. Possession of the remaining merchandise was instrumental in bringing me to my **BREAKING POINT**.

That night I was completely out of drugs and hit the street to sell the remaining items. I was desperate and needed a buzz...BAD. As weird as this may sound, as I walked the streets, I discerned a demonic spirit behind me breathing heavily. It seemed to be anxiously awaiting some upcoming event. It was as if I were halfway between the spirit world and this natural world. I overheard the conversations of several demons who were scheming to destroy me. I also detected a stronger, greater force present Who was restraining them. Despite this supernatural forewarning, I was determined to sell the stolen goods in my possession.

Then my worst nightmare began. I heard a voice call to me from a passing pickup truck.

"Hey, you!"

I instinctively began to run.

"Hey! Don't run, man. It's cool. It's just me," he yelled.

"Me who?" I asked nervously.

"The guy you tried to sell your stuff to earlier."

To my surprise it was. I calmed down and approached the truck. My attention was diverted to an unfamiliar person in the driver's seat. The first dude kept talking.

"This guy wants to buy the stuff you showed me earlier."

"I don't have it on me. I have to go pick it up," I told him.

"Hop in the truck and we'll get it together."

My mind was so clouded and deranged, I couldn't see the forest through the trees. I walked right into their trap.

The passenger door swung open and the man got out. He let me in the middle and climbed back into the truck. The door was closed and off we went. The three of us drove to where the stuff was stashed. They let me out, and I grabbed the goods. With merchandise in hand, I was strategically placed between them. We drove in complete silence for half an hour until I realized that the surroundings seemed very familiar. Then it hit me. I was in for the shock of my life. We were headed for the same house I stole the merchandise from.

The passenger's countenance changed as he broke the silence.

"Tonight's the night you die, junkie! We're gonna polish off the crack head who's been breaking into people's homes and stealing their stuff."

I was paralyzed with fear. I tried to shake myself out of the drugged stupor but to no avail. The house was just up the street. The truck pulled into the driveway. I realized that the guy who was driving was the son of the people who lived there. The father was totally enraged, and the mother was still crying over her stolen articles. This was the first time I saw the devastation of my victims.

I was violently yanked out of the truck and saw my life flash before my eyes. Then, out of the blue, someone cracked me in the back of my head with the butt of a shotgun. I fell to the ground, and the father repeatedly punched me in the face. I was dazed and confused. While I was on the ground writhing in pain, I overheard them talking about killing me. Paranoia struck me and I tried to escape. But I was too weak from the drugs I had consumed earlier in the day. I continued to squirm and struggle, but it was no use. I wasn't going anywhere. The driver had positioned my head face downward on the concrete with his foot so I couldn't see what they were doing. At that moment, I realized they were going to murder me.

I heard the son tell his father, "Do it! Get it over with already. Waste the mother f——!"

I felt the cold, hardened steel of the shotgun barrel against the back of my head. In a few seconds I was going to be a dead man. Believe it or not, this was only my intermediate **BREAKING POINT**.

A life is a terrible thing to waste. As I prepared for death, I remembered Jesus. Rather, He remembered me. Realizing the helplessness and hopelessness of the situation, I mustered up the last bit of strength I had and prayed.

"Lord, please forgive me for my sins so I can be with you in heaven."

At that very instant, everything changed. God moved and heaven intervened. My prayer authorized God to act on my behalf. A split second later, it was as if the Creator of the universe stepped in and said, "That's enough! No more! He belongs to **Me** now!" No one mentioned murder again. Instead, the three called the cops and held me until the police arrived. Thank God! I was never so ecstatic to see the men in blue. I was handcuffed, detained, and taken straight to jail. Praise the Lord! Prison was paradise compared to death and eternity in hell.

This was the first time in my life that I didn't mind going to jail. On the contrary, I welcomed it. I was so sick and tired of being controlled by cocaine that my mind and body needed a serious break. In actuality, I was just happy to be alive. I was placed in a cell and just lay there for hours. I slept, nursed my wounds, and thanked God for delivering me from that situation.

At that time, jail was exactly what I needed. I had suffered severe malnutrition from all the crack I had consumed. My body demanded major rest and lots of time to recuperate. I slept, awoke, and dozed off again. I enjoyed sleeping because it was an escape from the nightmare of reality.

Early the next morning I was escorted to the confined population. I stayed in the main unit for two days and was then taken to the annex. The annex was a separate division of the jail where they used plastic windows, steel doors, and concrete to detain the inmates instead of iron bars. The annex also has a special place in my heart. For it was there that the Holy Spirit began to reveal Himself to me. He showed me that I needed to make consistent godly decisions to turn my life around. I agreed and set specific time aside to pray. When I did, the other inmates in the unit laughed and mocked me. They said things like, "Nigga, get off your knees and stop faking with

God" and "We know you ain't serious and He knows it, too" and "Just another con from old, sly Fox."

I knew I was serious, and God knew I meant business. Therefore, I prayed habitually. Over time, I noticed that I still had a mean streak deeply rooted inside me. Even though I prayed daily, a part of me wanted to resume the free-for-all lifestyle of sin. It wasn't long before I conformed to my environment. Prison life never changes. It was still survival of the fittest. I picked fights with the new guys who came into my cell. I delivered the first punch because most of the time the first was the last. I fell back into the rut of unrighteousness. And I fell prey to the spirit of the prison system, which I call caged sin.

In order to get money during my prison stay, I communicated with many women on the outside. I reassured each one that she was the only woman for me. I promised to be different when I got out. I said anything to get money and keep it coming.

One day as I sat in my cell, I heard about Frank the garbage man who had gone legit. I envied him for making this positive move with his life. Little did I know that within a matter of months, he would go down on a 187 homicide charge. It was then that I was informed of Franky's story by a fellow inmate. He made an honest attempt to leave the fast life—but the fast life never left him.

Franky's Story

OVER THE YEARS, FRANKY AND CLINTON BECAME close friends. From time to time, they verbally expressed their differences, but for the most part, they were pals. Clinton occasionally picked fights with Franky because he was stronger and a better fighter. If push came to punch, Clinton knew he had the upper hand and could put Franky in his place if it was necessary.

One day Franky lost his cool and his head. He got tired of the routine vexation and pulled a sawed-off shotgun on Clinton. He stuck the nose of the barrel against Clinton's cheek and promised him instant death if he messed with him again. Clinton freaked and looked as if he had seen a ghost. The harassment stopped from that moment forward. Clinton had a new respect for Franky. It's amazing how a threat can renew the outlook of a friendship. However, there was something seriously wrong with this relationship. It was based on outdoing each other through violence.

Like so many other mindless punks I have already described, Clinton was known for shooting first and asking questions later. He survived by the trigger and had no respect for his victims—be they men, women, or children. It didn't matter who they were, just that they were hit or dead. If you crossed Clinton, he shot you. It was that simple. As carefree as Clinton was with his gun, Franky was just the opposite. He pistol-whipped people with his gun but never shot anyone. Many thought he was afraid to pull the trigger. Until one day—this day.

Franky and Clinton were partying together all day until about midnight. Later that same evening, they bumped into a seedy guy named Peter who had messed with Clinton in the past. Trouble was brewing and was about to spill over, for Clinton had already determined the next time Peter crossed him would be his last. In his mind, premeditated murder was already a done deal. Death patiently waited for its opportunity to strike.

Then it happened. Peter and Clinton began to exchange serious profanity. The argument was getting heated and hostile when Franky unexpectedly walked out of the club. Most thought he checked out. In actuality, Franky went to his car and got a 12-gauge, sawed-off shotgun. He loaded two cartridges into the barrel, hid it under his trench coat, and returned to the bar without saying a word.

During Franky's brief absence, Peter continued to harass Clinton. Unbeknown to Peter, Franky left and returned to the bar with the weapon.

Franky spoke up. "What are you hasslin' my homie for, man?"

"Butt out! This ain't between you and me," Peter said. "It's between me and Clinton. Move or you're gonna get hurt." Then Peter roughly pushed Franky out of the way.

That was the wrong thing to do because it set Franky off. Peter became an unsuspecting victim. Before he could turn around and walk away, Peter met his doom blindsided. The sound of a single gunshot blast echoed throughout the bar. Peter was projected into the air and slammed into the wall. He fell on his chest and died instantly. His insides were splattered all over the place. Blood and flesh were everywhere.

Franky walked over, stood next to the fresh corpse, looked down, and said, "Nigga, I told you not to mess with me! Now look at you. Stupid, freakin' fool." Then he left without saying another word.

Franky finally did it. He pulled the trigger. The worst part about it was that he had no remorse for his actions. In his mind, Peter started the situation, Franky just finished it. Society should have been gratified, for some might think it was rid of one more nemesis. In reality, he was just another lost soul.

The story ended, and my mind returned to the reality of my cell. I noticed the other guys smoking, swearing, playing cards, and jiving each other. This was the first time I felt like an outsider. I realized that I was being weaned from the mad life I was leading for some of the things I used to enjoy were now unattractive, repulsive, and downright sickening to me.

The following morning I saw Franky as I returned to the main jail. He shouted to me from a distance.

"Hey, Fox! What's up, nigga?"

"Hey, what's hanging, baby boy?" I asked, welcoming his comeback. "Franky, what are these crackers doin' to you?" I asked.

"Man...these fools are trying to throw the book at me. I never faced time like this before. They're talking about 35 years mandatory with 35 running wild!" he told me.

"Franky, I'd like to slap my hands upside your head! You're goin' down like a chump!" I yelled back.

"You don't wanna do that, Fox. Haven't you heard? I'm into killin' niggas now," he said.

Like Peter, I was blown away. I had to know more, so I bombarded him with a series of thought provoking questions.

"Hey Franky, was it really that easy to murder a man? Don't you value your freedom? Does the hurt you caused Peter's family mean anything at all? Is this what you've become—a cold-blooded killer?"

"It's too late. I can't change it. What's done is done. Now I face the consequences of my crime." That was all Franky had to say.

I asked Franky these questions to get answers. But I was really asking myself the same questions. This caused me to evaluate and reevaluate my life. My thoughts momentarily flashed back to my adolescence. I recalled the time I was 13 years old during church revival when the power of God changed my outlook on life. I remembered the overwhelming peace and endless joy I had with God. At that time, I never had a problem that was too big for Him to handle. God always reassured me that everything would be all right—and it was. As I relived those memories, I began to weep in my cell in full view of the other inmates. I felt an overwhelming need to fellowship with God. But at that point in my spiritual walk, I was willing to go only partway with God.

I stayed in the county jail for six months. Then I was sent to the new booking facility in Orlando because it was closer to Lakeland than Lake Butler. I was tried, found guilty, and sentenced to three- and one-half-years. I got off easy. This time the letter "B" was placed in front of my number. At that time, I was B-104853. This indicated that I was a convicted felon for the third time.

I became a permanent resident of the Orlando Correctional Prison. I worked in the kitchen to pass the longevity of the sentence. From time to time, I stole different items and pawned them just to have money in my pockets. Although I hadn't stopped stealing, I did cut back on the violent outbreaks. Change in my person was slow, but evident. In my mind I wanted to serve God. But my words and actions didn't always line up with my thoughts and desires. My spirit was willing, but my soul had other ideas and my flesh was incredibly weak.

During that three-and one-half-year period, I got involved with many types of hustlers. Most of them were pimps. I met a guy named Michael who was known as "Macka Roni." He had been a pimp for over 13 years. This brother was so slick that one time he left jail wearing his prison clothes and within a week he had 43 tailor-made suits in his closet. Macka Roni was as smooth as silk with every facet polished. He was the best street hustler I ever met or knew. I looked up to him because of his uncanny success. And I was excited about hanging with a guy like Roni. It was good to find a role model I could emulate.

When the opportunity presented itself, I walked over to him and said, "What's up, pimp?" His response took me totally by surprise.

"I ain't no pimp and don't call me one either."

I was shocked. "Nigga, what's wrong with you? Who rained on your parade?" He didn't answer. I wanted to know, so I pressed him for more info.

"Fox, about six months ago I tested positive for HIV. I got the disease because of my foolish lifestyle. I wish I gave up pimping and ho's before this happened, but I didn't. I was such a fool. Now I'm paying the price and someday soon I'm gonna die."

Macka Roni was doomed. Death was only a matter of time.

I was absolutely stunned by what I heard. I couldn't believe my ears. First Kenny, then Franky, and now Macka Roni. All of them blew their second chance at life—and regretted it. The only consoling words I said to him were, "Get saved. Only God can help you when everyone else fails."

That night in my cell, I thought about our conversation. I had compassion on Macka Roni, kneeled down, and interceded for him. This was a first. I actually prayed for God to save and heal him. Something inside me wanted Roni to know God and live. Later, I found out that *something* was actually *Someone*—the Holy Ghost. My attitude about others had changed. The heart of stone I acquired through sin was transformed into a heart of flesh. In the past I never cared about another human being. I was the center of my universe. But now I was praying and weeping for a fellow inmate.

Even though my conversion was genuine and I was now a child of God, I wasn't ready to live wholeheartedly for Jesus. He had my heart, but Satan and I still ruled the other parts of me. Consequently, it wasn't long before I was deceived away from Christ. It became increasingly clear that I needed some type of spiritual guidance. I had a lot of questions regarding the Bible, but no one to instruct me. Therefore, due to innocence and ignorance, I dismissed the Word of God as absolute truth and investigated other religions.

I looked into becoming a Muslim, but I couldn't take it seriously. Any group who believes the white man is the devil is asinine. Besides, I liked to eat pork and bacon. I wasn't about to give up a supposed "unclean pig" for a stupid religion. I also read about the prophet Muhammad. He didn't minister to me at all, so I kept looking. I was in dire search of a religion that wasn't as strict as Christianity. Somehow I stumbled across the Jehovah Witnesses, who were way off base scripturally. This entire religion is based on a lying wonder. As far as I was concerned, Joseph Smith of the Mormon Church had his vision while he was hallucinating on LSD. In time I came across a man named Angelo who was a psychic astrologer. He told me he could accurately predict the future. I told him he was full of it. I asked myself, "If Angelo was a genuine prophet, why didn't he foresee that he was going to get busted for selling drugs?" I didn't get any satisfaction from the religions I checked out. And I had it with the cults. Later, I discovered all of them were counterfeits.

One day during my kitchen work shift, I was introduced to a Haitian drug lord named Kennell. He was an illegal alien in search of what every hustler thinks will make him happy—"the American Dream." Kennell made great money selling drugs. He enjoyed baffling the police with voodoo and black magic. This brother lived carelessly and recklessly. For example, he told me of the time when he was stopped by the police with three kilos of cocaine in his front seat. The cops suspected something, but when they searched his vehicle they found corn instead of coke. Kennell duped the law. He was free to go, no further questions. Most drug dealers use the black arts to conceal their criminal operation and activities. The problem is that sorcery and voodoo don't last. The only loyalty Satan has to humanity is death—anyway possible—the sooner the better. A majority of the people who serve the devil through witchcraft end up either in prison or dead.

Kennell told me that voodoo revolutionized his hustling business. By invoking demons, his con went from $65 a day to more than $1,000 a day. I was impressed with his quick success and how he went from rags to riches. Because of my obsession with the occult, Kennell informed me that when we got out of jail I would be promoted to his first lieutenant. On account of this, I looked forward to the day when I could immerse myself in the workings of devils. Yet I had a dilemma. I was at a spiritual crossroad. In regard to evil, I had to go all the way or get out of the game completely. I chose the former despite the fact that God dealt with my heart. I pushed Him aside once more. God had to wait. I was not ready to relinquish all. Jesus was not the Lord of my life. I was going to sell drugs even if I had to shoot a dealer or occult priest to make it happen.

Kennell had seven days left on his sentence. Although he mentioned that the Department of Immigration was after him, we didn't dwell on that improbability. We had our sights set on bigger things—namely money, fame, and glory. To my surprise, three days before Kennell's release from prison, the immigration authorities caught up with him, captured him, and deported him to Haiti. Rumor has it that when the Haitian people take back a strayed citizen, that person is put to death—especially those involved in voodoo. Such was the fate of this magician from hell. The devil did with Kennell as he willed. This worker of iniquity was killed by his own master. Satan has no loyalty. Kennell was the fourth person who was sovereignly removed from my life. It was obvious that God shut the door on murder through Franky, pimping through Macka Roni, and Satanism through Kennell. Despite the hand of the Lord that resisted me, I wasn't ready to give up hustling.

A fellow prisoner named Chris told me about a "root man" who gave him good luck charms. Chris regularly contacted the witch doctor to find out about upcoming police raids so he wouldn't get busted for selling drugs. The reason Chris was in jail was because he blew off the warlock. Consequently, he got caught and was thrown in the slammer for three years.

At this point in my testimony, I want to relate another truth. Satan is an opportunist. He will scheme and strategize a person into committing sin. The devil will help you do wrong and then imprison you in the process. He'll coax you to think, speak, and act in an unlawful manner. When the gig's up, Satan and his demons will drop you like a hot potato and let you serve your "time." He first influences a person to sin. Then the devil abandons and condemns that person after he or she succumbs to his temptation. Satan is such a two-faced bastard. He is the worst traitor of all. If the devil betrayed God, how much more will he betray you?

Satan blinded my mind. Instead of seeing the outcomes of Franky, Kennell, and Chris, I was totally fascinated by the temporary fame and glamour of their lifestyles. I discovered the key to becoming a successful criminal and patiently waited for the opportunity to use it.

Time flew quickly. I finished my three-and one-half-year sentence in June of 1988, and was again released to my home—the streets. I was dumped off at the Orlando bus station. For some strange reason, I didn't take the first bus out. Rather, I decided to catch the midnight bus to Lakeland. Little did I know my delay was just another trick of the devil to throw me back into the joint.

I had several hours to kill, and a feverish lust burned in my loins. It had been 18 months since I enjoyed intimate female companionship. I had $100 in my pocket and all I could think about was drugs and getting it on with a fine woman. Sometimes, lust is picky.

While I waited, I hooked up with a brother who was also just released from prison. We struck up a conversation and he told me he knew where to find the finest women in the world. I had nothing to lose, time to kill, and sex to gain, so I joined him. We walked two blocks and saw our first prospect. Jennifer was very shapely and had beautiful eyes but was plagued with a drug problem. I played on her weakness to get what I wanted. I supplied her with drugs, and she yielded her body to me. I used her until lust had its fill. That's how it is on the streets. It's a virtual barter system. Money for drugs. Drugs for sex. Sex for money. Then the vicious cycle repeats itself all over again.

After I used and abused Jennifer, I tried to find the brother who I met at the bus terminal. Since I didn't know his name, I walked around and eventually found him in an alley with a bad case of "terrible jones." He was hurting so much he was intensely searching the ground for drugs that someone may have dropped. He saw me out of the corner of his eye and stood up.

"Man, I gotta do somethin' to get this monkey off my back."

"What ya got in mind?" I asked.

"Let's pull an easy gig and get some fast cash. We'll hit this junkyard three blocks down the street, strip some cars for parts, take them to old man Will, and hock 'em for money."

"Count me out. I want no part of that action," I told him. "Besides, I never broke into a junkyard before."

"You don't have to," he responded. "All ya gotta do is be my lookout and whistle if you see a troll rolling," he told me. I hesitated. He pressured me, and I responded against my better judgment.

"Okay," I agreed, "but it better work! This could cost us a lot more than we're willing to pay."

The three or four blocks we walked to the junkyard seemed like miles. When you're about to do a crime you know nothing about, time and distance become greatly exaggerated. It's like you're in slow motion. You take one step forward and two steps backward. I felt as if I were in a time warp—wandering aimlessly down this endless road. We finally arrived near the site, but it took forever.

As we approached the junkyard, we saw a broken-down fence in the distance. We stopped just outside the gate. The dude from Orlando gave the instructions.

"Wait here and watch for me."

I kept silent as he slid under the fence and vanished into the dark night. I nervously waited for about five minutes. I was getting very fidgety when all of a sudden I heard an obnoxious resounding BEEP...BEEP...BEEP! That noise wasn't good news. It was the burglar alarm. He unknowingly had tripped it off. Son of a b——! All I could think of was getting out of that place...NOW! I refused to go back to prison for a petty crime like this one. From a distance an all-too-familiar sight approached. Flashing red and blue lights. An all-too-familiar sound accompanied those lights that echoed throughout the surroundings. This dreadful sound penetrated my entire person at an accelerated pace. The whiny, whirling sound of a police siren is the worst sound in the world to a free con. I bolted that scene like a stallion on fire. I dashed into the back alley and faded into the depths of its blackness. I ran fast, hard, and as long as I could.

The sound of the siren faded and became distant. Thank God! Sweat dripped from my face more from fear than from my sprint. I beat the law and was still free. As I calmed down and caught my breath, I wondered what happened to the guy from Orlando. He probably was caught in the act, cuffed, and on his way back to the county jail. Better him than me. I ran again until I saw a familiar sign. The Greyhound bus station was visible in the distance. I was tremendously relieved to see that sign again. I had escaped the authorities and thwarted the plot of hell. That was way too close for comfort.

I sat in the bus station until I heard the announcement for my city. I boarded the bus with my carry-on bag and a beer. I sat in the back of the bus because I didn't want to be disturbed. I needed to chill, drink my brew, and calculate my next move. Due to the outcome of Macka Roni, I knew my pimping days were over. I put it to rest once and for all. I had finally grown up and learned from another's mistake. And I wasn't about to die for a piece of flesh. Despite this growth, I still desired to find a "root man" and sell drugs more than ever because the money was quick and easy.

Trying to Put Things Back Together

THE BUS DROVE AN HOUR AND STOPPED IN LAKELAND. It felt good to be a civilian again. I got off and went straight to my great-grandmother's house who was overjoyed to see me. She gave me a loving kiss and hugged me the way a mother embraces a wayward son. Her words of wisdom weren't foreign to me.

"Shawn, you need to do the right thing so you can stay out of jail."

A spontaneous "Yes, Momma" came out of my mouth. I agreed with my mouth, but my mind had a different agenda. The evil within wanted to do everything opposite what was good and right.

That night from my mother's kitchen telephone, I called Dr. Bradley, who was also known as "the Louisiana root man." I shared with him my dreams of success, riches, and power. I related my strategy to accomplish these things through dealing drugs. I asked him to work some magic to keep the cops off my tail until I cooled down. He agreed and told me to send him $50. He would whip up a "mojo" to do the trick.

The next day one of my longtime friends, Paul, introduced me to a dark-skinned woman named Sophia. Paul was currently dating Sophia's best friend, Dee Dee. He knew I was fresh out of jail, in need of company, and wasn't involved in any relationships. Sophia and I clicked immediately. She was the type that upon meeting her, you swore you knew her all of your life. Consequently, I opened up to her and shared about my past life. I also made it very clear that I had absolutely no intention of changing my present business. Sophia didn't have a problem with that. As long as I never brought drugs into her home or discussed them in front of her

9

son. I agreed. This was the first time in a long time that I was honest with a woman from the get go.

At that time, Sophia wasn't working. She and her son survived on child support and a monthly welfare check. Sophia repeatedly tried to convince me to go legit. She went as far as offering to get a job to take care of me. I was floored. My ego wouldn't allow me to have a woman support me. It was obvious that I needed serious mind renewal about relationships and the opposite sex. Besides, I was convinced the only job I could get would pay minimum wage. Who can survive on $4.85 an hour?

Sophia was consumed with making me happy. She lived for me and catered to my every whim. One day as we sat on the front porch, she got serious on me.

"Shawn, please don't hurt me," she said. "I can't handle it if you do. Too many men who I trusted in the past have almost destroyed me."

I looked her dead in the eye and said, "Don't be silly. I'll never hurt you." I lied right through my teeth. Hurt and pain was inevitable. I wondered if I could live up to her expectations. Only time would tell.

My relationship with Sophia was different from all of the others in the past. She had a great deal of respect for me and I had matured. Although she never said it, I believe Sophia loved me. I had a desire to settle down in a serious relationship. But there was only one problem. I wasn't ready to give up my present lifestyle for anyone—including God. For this reason, I knew it wouldn't work and we wouldn't last.

Late one night Sophia woke up and told me she had a dream about Jesus. He was hanging on the cross. Jesus asked Sophia if she loved Him. She answered, "Yes." That was the last thing I wanted to hear. When Sophia shared her dream with me, I knew God was dealing with both of us. I felt the frustration of the lie I was living. A spiritual tug-of-war existed between the two natures within me. Although God was seriously tugging at my heart, I was running as fast as I could in the opposite direction. I thought to myself, "Who is God that I should trust Him?" After all, I've never seen God, heard

Him, or felt Him. What I didn't realize was that the just live by faith. I tried to drown God's conviction through strong drink and crack. It didn't work. It never does. When the buzz and high wore off, the conviction was still present.

The following evening I was extremely drunk, high, and out of money. There was only one thing to do—resort to my old ways. A quick burglary would do the trick. I walked for about two miles and came upon a series of secluded town houses. Some had lights on, others were pitch-dark. I picked one out and knocked on the door. After several minutes and no answer, I concluded that no one was home. The front door had a dead bold lock, so I checked the windows. They were also locked. I had to break to enter, so I picked up a brick and shattered the window. Little did I know I was being watched. The break-in was so loud that I ran two blocks away to see what would happen. To my surprise, within a matter of minutes the place was swarming with cops.

Then I got cocky. In great stupidity, I walked over to one of the officers and struck up a conversation.

"What's goin' on?" I asked innocently.

"Someone tried to break into this condominium," he said.

Like a fool itching to be caught, I egged him on. "The crime in this city is way out of hand. It must be dealt with and stopped."

With that comment, I was off. Or so I thought. I attempted to walk away, but the cop asked me to join him at the window. Not to arouse any further suspicion, I complied without hesitation.

I didn't realize the next-door neighbor had witnessed the whole incident. But because the woman was older, she couldn't positively identify me. I was off the hook. Or so I thought. I started to walk away the second time when one of the officers looked down and noticed that my footprint matched the one underneath the window. Busted. I was abruptly thrown to the ground and handcuffed. The cops squeezed the cuffs so tightly my circulation was partially cut off.

I knew I was headed back to prison. This time I would be tried as a habitual offender and could be sentenced to 30 years. After the cops placed me in the back seat of their squad car, I called on the name of Jesus in great desperation. I expected an earthquake or some other type of cataclysmic event to liberate me. Nothing. Instead, I was taken to the local police station and charged with attempted burglary. I was then placed in a holding cell that reeked with the same unmistakable stench of urine.

Back behind bars, I thought to myself, "Will this cycle of destruction ever end? Will a man fight against his Creator and win?" NO! In the midst of that cell, in front of many curious onlookers, I fell to my knees. I was at the point in my life when my endurance and self-control totally collapsed under pressure. I had reached my final **BREAKING POINT**. This was the first time that I was really serious with God. I cried out to Him from a genuine heart. I fell upon the Rock of Salvation and was broken—on the inside—within my spirit, my heart, my mind, my soul, and my will. Like the mind-blinded Saul of Tarsus, I finally surrendered. I had enough. I stopped rebelling, bucking, and running. The battle was over and I lost. As a result, my nightmare from hell ended.

My sincerity changed my present and redirected my future for all eternity. God set me on a new course—His course—both spiritually and naturally. I was totally transformed during that minute of prayer. My past failures no longer mattered. How could they? They were gone! The blood of Jesus cleansed me from all sin and iniquity. As a result, I was engulfed in the glory of the Lord. Nothing else mattered but God. He was real as never before. Old things were passed away and I was a brand new creature in Christ.

In the past, when I tried to make it by myself, life always resulted in failure, grief, and sorrow. Now I tried my last hope. What I didn't realize was that God was not only my last hope, He was my best hope and my only hope. Everything changed because I finally came clean with God through an honest, heartfelt prayer. Returning my life to my Maker on that bare, cement, jail floor was the best decision I ever made. I called upon God for the first time in two decades and He answered me. A simple, sincere prayer engaged heaven on my behalf. I was instantly delivered from the destruction of sin and eternity in hell.

I was escorted back to the main jail in Bartow. Because my

conversion was genuine and God dwelled in me, I had a completely different outlook on life. After all, I was *now* accepted in the beloved by Abba Father. Consequently, I removed myself from hellish activities and walked away from confrontational violence. They were beneath me. I refused to stoop to their level. Besides, I had better things to do with my time such as read the Word of God. For the first time in my life, I had hope and purpose. I was created for a reason and God had a plan for my existence.

I was sick and tired of the old ways of living. I desperately wanted a better, more fulfilling life. Although I had a new beginning, I needed a fresh start. I asked God to have mercy on me and He did. I was wrong and repented for my evil ways.

As the day of my trial and sentencing approached, the state's attorney gave me the lowdown. It was highly probable that I would be convicted as a repeat offender. This meant three long decades in prison. The thought of being locked up for 30 years blew my mind. When the anxiety of the future and the unknown attacked me, prayer and meditation in the Psalms comforted me. These vehicles reassured me that God was in control. He was now my Father and I was now His son. (It felt great to finally have a Father.) God would deal with me as He saw fit. In reality, there was nothing I could do about it. My life and destiny were in the trustworthy hands of the Almighty.

I stayed at Bartow for two weeks and was then sent back to the Annex. The routine got very redundant. This time I viewed the jail from a different perspective. Something changed. The place and people were the same but I was different. Prison was like a human zoo that caged fleshly animals. The place was a madhouse. Hell City. Violence was in full manifestation all around me. Men were beaten, abused, gang raped, and suffered every other vile act you could imagine. The atmosphere was so barbaric that the first thing I did was pray. God and I knew that I wasn't going to last or survive in this den of devils without His help. I prayed for solitary isolation because I didn't know if I could live for God with all of this evil about me. My request was denied. I was stuck. So I read the Bible more than ever, prayed harder, and meditated on the Scriptures day and night.

No one in jail encouraged me. I was totally on my own. But with the Holy Ghost, I didn't need anyone else. Most of the other cons told me I was wasting my time. As far as they were concerned, it was too late to get religious or spiritual. Demons through them regularly harassed me. They said that God wasn't going to help and the system was going to throw the book at me. I laughed in their faces and told them the devil is a liar.

One week later Max, one of my homies from New York, came into my cell. It was good and bad to see him. He looked as if he had been mugged and beaten by a gang. His eyes had deep cuts under them and were almost swollen shut. I shared my spiritual experience with Max. I told him that I had finally given up the fast life and was on a desperate search for God. After much discussion, he told me he wanted Christ in his life too. I led him to the Lord right there, in the middle of my cell.

Transforming the Zoo into an Ark

THE ANNEX WAS DIVIDED INTO WINGS. EACH WING contained several different dormitories. Each dormitory contained eight different cells. Max and I were placed in Dorm A, Cell 5. Unfortunately, our cell was full of hoodlums who defiled everyone with their profane speech. One brother actually used the "f" word to complete an entire sentence, which is grammatically impossible. These cons ministered everything *but* grace to my ears. They didn't give a lick about life—be it theirs or another's. Their main concern was the infliction of bodily harm to someone else. Many of the cons knew me from my previous visits, but they didn't realize that I was now saved. Because my past reputation proceeded me, they didn't try to chump me off.

In spite of all the demonic activity happening around us, Max and I kept our focus. Daily we prayed, read our Bibles, and fellowshipped. As a result, we weren't conformed to the prison world, but were transformed by renewing our minds with truth. Our nonconformity caused the Gospel to appeal to the other inmates.

Max cut hair to make extra money. He learned how to cut letters into the scalp. I thought this would be a good witnessing tool, so I had him inscribe Scriptures like John 3:16 in my hair. This caused quite a stir. When brothers approached me for an explanation, I whipped out my miniature pocket Bible and told them about the love of God. The Lord Jesus Christ was boldly proclaimed to anyone who would listen. Many were subconsciously reformed to God.

10

Max and I continually interceded for ourselves and others. I can honestly say that because of our prayers, the atmosphere changed within our cell and throughout the entire dormitory. I noticed that we were having an impact on the other inmates. When Max and I knelt and prayed, the others followed our lead and did the same. This was a very big deal because my cell contained the worst offenders in the entire Annex. Through the love and power of God, in two weeks' time the entire cell gave their lives to Christ. God used me—Shawn Mosley—in prison—to save all eight men in my cell. You talk about miracles...this was it! Praise God! Afterward, the eight of us gathered daily to pray and sing songs. The presence of God was so strong that the guards constantly avoided our cell because the Spirit of holiness convicted and repelled them.

One day during our devotional time, a rough, tough brother named So Bad came into our cell. Rumor had it that he beat many men to death with his bare hands. At the young age of 17, So Bad did time at the "Rock," which is an extension of the big house at the Florida State Penitentiary. So Bad was a solid mass of flesh who weighed every bit of 300 pounds. However, his mind didn't match his physique. He was a child in a man's body. So Bad was nothing more than an oversized bully who didn't realize he was about to join our fellowship.

At that time, I didn't know if inducting So Bad into our group was such a good idea. Later, I found out it was. We had our Bible study and testimonial service as usual. I was about to conclude the service when So Bad unexpectedly took the floor. My heart pounded harder in apprehension of what was going to happen. The Holy Spirit comforted me, so I relaxed and trusted God. What I heard baffled my ears and bewildered my mind. When So Bad opened his mouth, he spoke in the most innocent voice I ever heard from a man that size. He shared with the group the time he was robbing a stranger when the victim pulled out a gun and attempted to kill him. The man fired seven shots at So Bad within point-blank range, but every bullet missed. It was impossible for the stranger not to hit such a large target. He told us that God must have been present and intervened to have survived that near-death experience. So Bad never forgot that incident. Now he wanted to be on God's side. It turned out that So Bad wasn't so bad after all. No man is so bad that God can't accept, love, or change him. So Bad accepted Jesus Christ into his heart as his personal Lord and Savior.

During the days and weeks that followed, I empathized with Paul the Apostle who experienced great difficulty convincing the first century Christians of his genuine conversion. Although I was naturally apprehensive about So Bad, I had a spiritual peace in my heart. The fact of the matter is that God doesn't want anyone to perish, but all to come to the knowledge of repentance. I wanted this brother to have a fair chance at the Gospel, so we took him in. If God accepted So Bad, who was I to reject him? We openly received this new convert and he became a part of our fellowship. His physical size and strength lent credibility to the move of God.

In a matter of weeks, 26 men were attending our daily fellowship. Twenty six out of 44 wasn't bad; it was over 50 percent. Fifty nine percent to be exact! One by one, I saw the men develop a sincere desire for salvation. They attended our fellowship, anticipating God to move and bless. He never disappointed us.

As I complied with the Bible and the leading of the Holy Ghost, God again mediated on my behalf. God began His second gracious work. Through a series of miraculous events, judge after judge reduced my prison sentence from 30 years to 17 years to 9 years. God knew I couldn't fulfill my sentence without His supernatural help. Jesus was a friend who stuck closer to me than a brother. And the Holy Spirit comforted me at every turn. All that really mattered was that I was on God's side. He was my peace, my strength, my life, my everything.

After six months in jail, I received a "Dear John" letter from Sophia. The gist of it was she still cared but couldn't wait for me any longer. She met an honest, working man who didn't sell or use drugs. At first, I was hurt. But then I realized I was to blame. The bottom line was I was wrong. Losing Sophia was the price I paid for being a criminal. I gave the situation to God because my hands were tied. Maybe He had someone better planned for me.

Max and I continued our fellowship until he went to court. The judge was extremely merciful to Max also. He faced a probable long sentence, but received only three years. Afterward, he was sent back to the main jail. Max continued his evangelistic outreach in the central prison. He wrote to me periodically and related that the fire of God was ablaze, catching, and spreading in his area.

A few weeks later, it was my turn...again. I went before the court for another sentencing. As I wondered what the ruling would be, one Scripture kept coming to mind. *"He which hath begun a good work in you will perform it until the day of Jesus Christ...."* I expected God to finish the miracle He began earlier. After all, He is faithful that promised. Then God moved. The pending term of 9 years that was strongly recommended by the state's attorney was rejected. Yesss! Instead, the judge sentenced me to 5 years with 8 months actual time served. Eight months! What a godsend! Praise the Lord! My sentence of 9 years was reduced to 5 years to less than 1 year—8 months—all in a matter of months. God speedily delivered me from **29** years of institutional life. Hallelujah!!! I had great reason to celebrate, for I witnessed an incredible miracle that day. Proverbs 21:1 says, *"The king's heart is in the hand of the Lord...he turneth it whithersoever he will."* This means God turns the heart of man however He wants to. Surely, God's hand leaned heavy upon the judge that day, who was merely a tool of salvation.

I returned to the Annex and packed my belongings. I was ecstatic by the outcome of the day. I couldn't believe what was happening. God gave me a new lease on life. As I departed the main prison, many of the new converts lined up to see me off. I had a lump in my throat and noticed a mist in some of their eyes. Some I greeted, some I hugged. We wished each other well and Godspeed. Thanks to the mercy and grace of my newfound Heavenly Father, everything was finally going in the right direction. My life took a turn for the better because I did. Thank you Jesus!

I was sent back to the main jail for one week. There I was again exposed to its ongoing violence. I hated that place and looked forward to going to prison. Let me explain. In prison, you have the option of removing yourself from evil and vice. If a disagreeable situation occurs, a con can either get involved or remove himself from the raucous by retreating to the other end of the compound. In prison, I wouldn't be placed in a room with five deranged men. Instead of being confined to a 12 foot by 12 foot cell crammed with many others, I would have a cell all to myself. That way I would not be defiled or affected by their sins. These were just some of the reasons why I looked forward to going to prison as opposed to staying in jail.

My stay in the county jail went by very quickly. Time flies when you're having God. Before I knew it, I was back in the prison van, which was headed down that old familiar road. I was on the path of unrighteousness in route to the Orlando Correctional Center to be booked in again. Despite the obvious similarities, this trip was different from the last in one sense. It had hope. After a lifetime of downhill struggles, battles, and hell, I was finally headed uphill. I also experienced an incredibly fulfilling peace in my spirit. This was accompanied by an internal joy that flowed from within. The peace and joy of God reassured me that everything was going to be all right.

As I gazed through the steel bars welded to the van windows, I realized that I was imprisoned in my own little world. The outside environment was open and free, but I was in bondage. The world of life and liberty appealed to me much more than the world of death and prison. I enjoyed the radiant beauty of life's simplest things. The beautifully blooming trees. The billowy white clouds. The life-giving sun. And the earth glimmering in its summer glory. On the way to Orlando, the van passed many farms. I perceived horses, their mares, and the cattle on a thousand hills. These aspects of nature thrilled me because I saw God in everything I observed. My perspective changed because I now had Christ in my life. As a result of my born again experience, a brand new world opened up to me. The world of life. I enjoyed the earth, its creatures, and life for the very first time. I was so elated that God spared me. And I was happy just to be alive.

The bus arrived at the Orlando Correctional Center sooner than I expected. Once I was there, checking in became old hat. I went through the usual procedures. Some of the guys I met during my previous visits were still there. Unlike me, they weren't going anywhere and I was just passing through. For example, there was this believer named Henry Walker who witnessed to me in the past. The love of God rested upon this Brother in great abundance. So much so that it actually repulsed me prior to my spiritual conversion. I remember one of our past conversations when I told Henry I wasn't about to serve "the white man's God. At that time, I was so embittered and full of hate I threatened to break his neck if he ever approached me again with his talk of God.

This time when I saw Henry, I embraced him as my beloved Brother in the Lord. This is biblical, for *"There is neither Jew nor Greek...for ye are all one in Christ Jesus."* All people are equally baptized into the Lord's Body at the moment of salvation. And they who are joined unto the Lord are one Spirit. I thank God that the color of a man's skin is not a stumbling block to the Trinity. The fact of the matter is if a person has a skin problem, he or she also has a sin problem. People in the world will find and create reasons to hate each other. On the contrary, God's people must make a conscious decision to love all people regardless of a person's sex, age, race, or social-economic group. Disciples of Christ must focus on the *contents* of the package, not the *wrapping*. With God, it's who and what is on the inside that counts.

Henry was elated to know that I was saved and living for God. My spiritual transformation actually brought tears to his eyes. Later, I found out that God had instructed him to intercede for me. In doing so, Henry manifested God's agape love, which flowed from the throne room of heaven to his circumcised heart to me. He was very instrumental in my salvation.

Henry and I immediately hooked up. When we did, both of us knew that a divine connection had taken place. We prayed together and served God with all of our hearts. One day Henry gave me a book that revolutionized my life. The book was entitled *The Cross and the Switchblade*. The story was set in the streets of New York City. It described a young man named Nicky Cruz who ruled the area as the leader of a Latin gang. The narrative speaks of a young country pastor who was commissioned by God to end gang violence in that region. The meeting of pastor and gang leader was a classic confrontation between good and evil. As always, God prevailed.

The gang leader described in this book reminded me of myself. I related to Nicky Cruz. He had no role model at home. He was on the streets at an early age. He was directed and dictated to by society. He caved in to peer pressure. And he was in continual trouble with the law. Some parts of the book made me cry. Others caused me to rejoice. *The Cross and the Switchblade* hit home on all accounts. It had a great impact on me, second only to the Bible. Jesus Christ was my spiritual role model, and Nicky Cruz quickly became my natural role model. That book confirmed a truth I already knew and believed—a "nobody" like me is someone "special" to God.

That night, I prayed during my private time.

"Jesus, give me what Nicky Cruz has. He was a drug addict, pusher, and gang banger just like me. Lord, you helped him. Please do the same for me. I know You're no respecter of persons. Just help me. Even if You have to send me a country preacher like David Wilkerson. Do whatever it takes. I trust You."

When I finished my prayer, I knew that heaven heard me. God responded by appointing and mobilizing a fleet of angels on my behalf.

One night while I was in my dormitory during lock down, something surprisingly supernatural happened. I felt inspired to get on my knees and pray. It was very late and the prison had settled down to near silence. My effectual, fervent prayer availed me much. After about an hour of intense intercession, I was baptized in the Holy Ghost. At first the language seemed weird. It was foreign to my ears. As I persisted and continued to speak in tongues, a soothing, invisible heat enveloped my person. When that happened, my entire body began to shake uncontrollably. God's presence was very strong, and His person was almost tangible. The baptism of the Holy Spirit felt like God Himself were breathing on me. In essence, He was through the Holy Spirit. I couldn't believe the life-giving Spirit of God visited *somebody* like me. I was overwhelmed and overjoyed. Although I didn't know how to properly receive the visitation, God overlooked my ignorance and blessed me anyway. He respected, honored, and fulfilled my desire for more of Him.

From that night on, before I went to sleep I covered myself with a blanket and communed with the Holy Spirit by speaking in tongues. The heavenly language produced a great internal heat that caused me to perspire. In the process the fire of God burned away much ungodliness in my life. Although this may sound strange, I actually fell in love with the presence of God and His baptism of fire.

I stayed in Orlando for three weeks. When my time was completed, I was sent to the Walton road prison in the Florida Panhandle. My first impression of the Walton Correctional Facility was chaos. The staff were restoring the base from the aftereffects of a major riot that had taken place two weeks earlier. The tension of that event still dominated the atmosphere. After the uproar and attempted breakout, 50 inmates were sent to a maximum security prison.

During my first couple of days at Walton, I observed some very unusual behavior. I watched inmate after inmate confront and challenge the administration. It was obvious that they had no respect for the commanding officers. The prisoners continually threatened the guards. This wasn't good because threats lead to rebellion. Rebellion, in turn, causes unnecessary violence, which brings about injury and death. Despite this pervasive attitude, I kept my focus on God and good. I liked Walton because it was a work prison. As long as I did my job, I was hassle free. If I complied, there was no unnecessary harassment from the enforcers. If I didn't, I had big problems.

What I disliked about work was that it took me away from God. I had a burning desire to know Him and all I wanted to do was read the Bible. Throughout the week I worked hard, lived right, and studied the Word of God. On Saturday I rested. On Sunday I attended all of the church services. When there was any downtime, I listened to sermons on the radio. I relished the messages about the blood of Jesus and His unconditional love.

As time went on, Walton Correctional Facility began to loosen up. The prisoners calmed down, personnel relaxed, and the guards resumed their normal status. Order was restored and everyone breathed a much needed sigh of relief. The threat of a hostile takeover decreased and ended. Prison life is easier to handle in times of peace, especially for a new convert like me. If the troublemakers had stayed, the situation would have gotten ugly and I could have reverted to my old ways. But that didn't happen. Neither God nor I wanted trouble. The goal was to stay clean and do the right thing.

Doing right is accepted by the world's standard. But in prison, it's just the opposite. Doing right is often mistaken for weakness. I learned the hard way that an inmate must never show any signs of weakness. Weakness often leads to abuse, violence, and death. Every prison has a handful of cons who prey upon the innocent and devour the unsuspecting like animals. They go about as roaring lions seeking whom they may devour.

Because I was now a child of God, it was His responsibility to preserve and protect me. He never let me down. I saw God's hand continually move on my behalf. He quickly removed me or my adversary from problems and serious threats. Therefore, I trusted in God's supernatural protection. For the duration of my sentence, God was always with me. He never left me or forsook me at any time.

About three months into my term, one of my cohorts from the street was sent to Walton. Harold was a tall, dark-skinned Brother who was graced with a happy-go-lucky attitude. He was the type of person who had a good outlook on life. Looking back, I know Harold was sent by God to reveal the next spiritual door upon my release. He told me about a place called Teen Challenge where new believers learned about Jesus Christ. Teen Challenge was a type of "Christian detox center" where losers, cons, pimps, prostitutes, and drug abusers were weaned of the world's vices. Candidates had to take the curriculum very seriously.

Harold shared about his enrollment and voiced his disapproval for not finishing the program. In retrospect, Harold wished he would have stuck it out. When he said that, I was reminded of a verse from Scripture. *"No man, having put his hand to the plough, and looking back, is fit for the kingdom of God."* Even though Harold didn't complete the program, I discerned the beneficial impact it had upon his person and life.

Concerning Harold and Teen Challenge, one question flashed into my mind. Why did he fail? Harold explained about the divine conviction and demonic condemnation he experienced during that intense period. At times it was too much for him to handle. Or so he was led to believe by the devil. Consequently, Harold bought the evil deception, made a bad decision, quit the program, and walked away from God. He didn't realize that God wouldn't allow him to be tempted beyond what he could handle. If Harold had stuck it out, God would have showed him the way of escape or delivered him from the tormenting demons.

As Harold explained this, it was almost as if God spoke directly through him to me.

"Shawn, the main reason I backslid was because I had the Word of God in my mind, but I didn't apply it to my life on a continual basis. This nullified God's Word in my life and made it void."

For some predetermined reason, Harold's words stayed in my mind. I was certain that God deliberately brought him across my path to reveal and speak this truth to me. In the days that followed, I meditated upon them often.

The Good News

11

MY TIME AT WALTON ALSO WENT QUICKLY. AS THE DAY of my release approached, I spent more time with God, reading and meditating upon His Word.

Every morning at eight o'clock we went to work. I was assigned to the sod squad. This work detail was incredibly monotonous. First we went to a big field to cut and remove grass from the ground. Then the sod was carried by hand through the front gate and laid throughout the compound. This process continued all day long until 5:00 p.m. Afterward, the inmates headed back to the dormitories, washed up, and prepared for "chow" in the mess hall.

When dinner was over, we returned to our assigned dormitories and waited for the daily mail delivery. I hated this time because I never received any mail. Sophia and I had gone our separate ways. We were no longer communicating and no one else cared. Even my own flesh and blood didn't realize how lonely I was. My mother was not the type of person who communicated through written correspondence. If she had something important to tell me, it was easier for her to pick up the telephone and call. This is why I never looked forward to letter time. The truth of the matter was I was jealous of the men who had relationships with people on the outside and heard from them on a regular basis.

One day when the mail was being distributed, the C.O. called my name. I was shocked. I actually received mail. He walked over to the cage and handed me a letter. It was from my sister Melissa. I couldn't believe it. It had been eight years since I last heard from her. With anxiousness and great anticipation, I ripped open the envelope. What I read was confirmation of yet another miracle. To my amazement, Melissa was saved and serving God. She informed me that Jesus Christ was now her personal Lord and Savior. Melissa vividly expressed the newfound joy she experienced. Truly, salvation was the best decision of her life. As it was mine.

As children, Melissa and I were very close. We were middle children and she was two years older than I. Both of us felt the rejection of our home and the void caused by our father's absence. Consequently, we considered ourselves the black sheep of the family. This propelled us into the fast lane together. Melissa was responsible for introducing me to alcohol. She and a friend gave me my first beer. And as you already know, it was all downhill from there.

The road to hell has many paths. Wide is the gate that leads to destruction. The patterns our lives took were almost identical. My past consisted of being a renowned drug addict, thief, pimp, and con man. Melissa's past consisted of being a drug addict, thief, prostitute, and con woman. Both of us were on our way to hell until the Lord intervened. Thank you, Jesus! The beauty of it is we both received Christ into our hearts and He turned everything around. Jesus was the best thing that could have happened to us. He is gloriously life-changing, to say the least.

The content of her letter deeply touched my heart. In addition to salvation, Melissa also revealed she was currently enrolled in the Teen Challenge program at western Michigan. I couldn't believe it. She related that it was a very positive environment. The facility was a healthy place for new believers to grow, discover their true identity in Christ, and enter into God's will. Melissa strongly suggested that I attend the program upon my release. I wasn't too dense to realize that God was trying to tell me something. Over a few months and through two or three witnesses, God's plan was established. First Harold. Then Melissa. Who would be next?

Despite the two confirmations, I debated within myself. My first thought was, "Once I get out of here, I ain't goin' to no rehab center." My second thought confirmed the first, "I'm sick and tired of state programs." What I really wanted to do was join a good church and get involved in ministry.

After 12 long months of incarceration, my release date finally arrived. Yesssss! Then it happened. On April 11, 1989, at the age of 23, I made history. I walked out of the prison gates for the last time...never to return again. I was reformed by God, not man, through love, not law or punishment. I said good-bye and left my past behind. Once again I experienced liberty. Ahhhh...the joy of freedom and being set free. I left the Walton Correctional Facility a changed man. I had a completely different outlook on life and a brand new perspective on everything else.

A vehicle arrived promptly at 8:00 a.m. to transport me to the local bus stop. As I cautiously approached the van, memories of the past haunted my mind. Was this it? Was I really changed? Would I be back? Did I really turn over a new leaf? That same instant, I realized I squandered **7** years during my four stays in the Florida State Prison system. What a waste of life and time—mine! I was such a fool. God gave me the gift of life and I tried to throw it away time and again!

When I entered the prison system, I was assigned the number 104853. Upon my departure, I had a different number, C-104853. The "C" indicated that I had been convicted of four different crimes. Through the process of temptation, trial, and error, I remained in bondage to the prison system. This changed at the moment of my salvation when I was translated out of darkness into the Kingdom of Light. During the beginning stages of my Christian walk, the enemy tried to deceive me. He attacked my mind and told me I was a four-time loser for the devil. This was true, but old things were passed away. A second later, God countered that thought and revealed I was now a one-time winner in Christ.

As I walked toward the van, the reality and revelation of freedom hit me hard. I realized I was finally free from the natural prison system and the spiritual prison system called "sin." Truly, when Jesus Christ makes someone free, that person is free indeed. This meant I was no longer a prisoner to anyone or anything. I had been liberated from sin, sickness, destruction, death, hell, demons, and Satan himself. Knowing the truth made me free. I was free because God liberated me from prison and Jesus the Truth lived in my heart.

Before I took my first step onto the van, I glanced back one last time at prison surroundings. The impossible barricade. The high walls. The barbed wire. The gun tower. The loaded machine guns. And the nervous guards. By my own choosing, prison became my home for many years. It was literally a house of hell.

That first step was huge. It was one small step for mankind, but one giant step for Shawn Mosley. I lifted my right foot, planted it firmly on the first step, strengthened my leg and back muscles, and pushed myself forward. I was thrust free from the clutching grip of the devil. I was finally delivered from the birth canal of sin. The cross was before me, the past was behind me. There would be no turning back. I climbed aboard the vehicle that was destined to shuttle me to my new life. I sat quietly and thanked Jesus silently that it was over—once and for all! Hallelujah!

I arrived in Lakeland, Florida, three hours later. I didn't have a place of my own to stay, so I went over to my brother's house. Derrick was very happy to see me. It had been many moons since our last visit.

"Hey, Fox. What's up, man?" he asked.

"Nothin' much, big bro'. I just turfed and am looking for a place to crib. Know any? Is there a chance you could house an X-con?" Derrick laughed because he understood my sense of humor.

"No problem, lil' bro'. Say no more." Then he gave me a firm brotherly embrace.

He continued, "It's good to see you, man. You're lookin' like new money. Fresh, clean, and ready for action."

"You ain't lookin' too bad yourself," I responded. "Except, you need a good shave."

Derrick gestured with his hand. "Come on in. Annette will be glad to see you."

Upon entering my brother's house, I was greeted by my sister-in-law.

"Hello, Shawn. How are you?" she asked.

"Much better than I was a few hours ago. I just got out of the pen and feel really good and clean."

We sat around and reminisced about old times and our childhood. It wasn't long before I was confronted with my first test. The enemy began his temptation through Annette. It's just like Satan to use a woman.

"Hey, brother-in-law, I've got an extra pack of cigarettes on my dresser. They're yours for the asking and taking."

"No thanks, sis'. I don't smoke anymore."

Derrick interjected, "That's good because it's a nasty habit. Man was never intended to smoke." I was surprised that Derrick came to my defense.

Round one was over. God and Shawn were still in control. Satan quickly regrouped for round two. This time he used a different person and another approach. Derrick left the room and returned with a cold Budweiser.

"Hey, lil' bro'. There's a whole case of Bud in the fridge. Help yourself."

I resisted the temptation. I was resolved not to bend or cave in to family or peer pressure. "Thanks, but no thanks. I don't drink anymore either," I said.

Derrick continued, "Man, I gave up everything but drinking. From now on, it's just me and my old pal Bud."

Round two was over. The bad guys were defeated and the good guys had the victory. Good God, bad devil. I passed both tests with flying colors. In the process, I learned how to say "no" in the face of sin.

Derrick recognized something different about me. He verbalized what he sensed.

"So, lil' bro'...I see you've made some changes in your life." The door of opportunity to witness to my older brother swung wide open. It was time to present the Gospel.

"No, I haven't. I accepted Jesus into my heart and He made the changes. Derrick, everything Momma ever said about Jesus is true. He died, was raised from the dead, and is alive forevermore! I have surrendered my life to Him. The Lord spared me from death three different times. He gave me several second chances at life and I'm not about to blow it," I said.

To my dismay, Derrick was supportive. With genuine sincerity he said, "Shawn, I'm really happy to hear that!"

The spiritual seed was sown.

Derrick changed the subject. "I spoke with Momma today on the telephone. She's coming over to visit. Sometimes I'm happy to see her and other times I'm not. Especially when she reminds me of Pop."

"What do you mean?" I asked.

"She's always trying to convert me. I've told her a hundred times that I'm not ready to be saved."

"Derrick, the only reason Momma tells you about Jesus is because she loves you. She wants you to experience the blessed and prosperous life she has because of Christ."

"Well...maybe you're right. But I've got to make that decision for myself. I don't want her pressuring or pushing me into something."

"That's true. But remember, Momma is gonna be herself and nobody is gonna change that," I said.

I conversed with Derrick for several hours. I glanced at the clock and it was after 6:00 p.m. Time flies when you're free! No sooner than I had lost focus of the clock, I heard a car horn outside. I walked to the window, pulled the curtains back, and caught a glimpse of Momma getting out of the car. Like an excited child, I darted to the door and met her on the front porch. It was the first time I had seen my natural birth mother in six years. I was elated to see her. The feeling was mutual. I gave Momma a sincere, heartfelt hug. I felt love and great comfort in her arms.

When the initial excitement faded, she asked me about my future plans. "What are you going to do with your life, son?"

"As of this moment, I really don't know. But I am gonna do the right thing from here on out," I responded. "Momma, did you know that I accepted Jesus Christ as my personal Lord and Savior?"

"Yes, son, I know. The joy of the Lord is all over your face. You made the right decision and I'm very happy for you," she replied. "Shawn, if you haven't made any plans regarding your future, I have a suggestion."

"Oh, really?" I asked excitedly. "Tell me about it. I'm all ears." I didn't expect to hear what she had to say.

"How about giving Teen Challenge a chance?"

As soon as my mother said that, I knew this was where God

wanted me to be. My fate was sealed. There was no way of getting around it or out of it. I was headed for Teen Challenge—like it or not. My destiny was revealed and confirmed by God's three witnesses.

"Okay, Momma. I'll give it a chance. How long is the program?"

"One year. I challenge you to give it a chance for at least six months. After that, if you don't want to stay, my door is always open as long as you serve God."

"It's a deal," I said.

"I'll come back tomorrow and pick you up. We'll buy you a one-way bus ticket and you'll leave on the 6th of May," she said.

"Sounds great to me," I said.

Momma got back in her car and drove away. Apparently, the only reason she came over was to get me to commit to Teen Challenge. It worked. I stopped fighting and gave in. God, my Heavenly Father, knows best!

Back on the Bus

12

THE DAY OF MY DEPARTURE WAS UNUSUALLY WARM IN the sunshine state. The temperature was nearly perfect. It wasn't too hot and it wasn't too cool. The outside conditions were just right, with a breezy, westerly wind cooling my skin. The clouds assisted the wind by billowing and shielding the blazing sun. This continued all day until six o'clock when Momma and I finally concluded the drive and arrived at the bus station.

Twenty one days had passed since I walked out of the correctional facility. Although it seemed like yesterday, life was moving along quickly. I was on a different path: a divine path, a predestined path, a chosen path that led to one place and one place only—Teen Challenge. This ministry was located in the small town of Muskegon, Michigan.

During the drive, a reoccurring thought plagued my mind. "Why in the world am I going to some hick town in the middle of nowhere?" Demons told me I wasn't going to like the place. Without proper discernment, I would have believed them. Besides, the name neither impressed nor challenged me. Regardless, deep down inside, the Holy Spirit demanded change.

As we drove into the bus station, Momma and I were silent for a short period. We quietly waited for the scheduled transportation to arrive. I utilized this time to collect my thoughts and mentally prepare for the challenge ahead. After many minutes, the bus pulled into the terminal. A voice on the loudspeaker informed all travelers of the boarding instructions. The voice was male, indifferent, and blaringly loud.

"Now loading in zone number two. All passengers from Winter Haven, Florida, to Detroit, Michigan. Climb aboard. Bus leaves in five minutes."

A mass of humanity rushed to the front entrance. I didn't have a lot of time and I wasn't about to miss God. I hugged my mother and gave her a loving, lasting embrace.

"Momma, please pray for me."

"Every day, son. I promise."

"I love you," I said.

"I love you too, son," she replied. "Expect God to bless and He will."

I extended my right hand to my stepfather and gave him a firm handshake. Without another word, I grabbed my overnight bag and proceeded toward the bus. I quickly got in line before I changed my mind.

This was the first time I entered a bus with the expectation of doing something positive with my life. It felt good for a change. As a matter of fact, it was the first time since the Job Corps that I had a positive mind-set.

I picked the first seat I came upon, in the front row near the window. I desired a window seat so I could wave good-bye to my family and enjoy the country scenery. The bus driver slammed the door shut, released the parking brake, and put the pedal to the metal. We were off. There was no turning back.

I retreated into my seat, got comfortable, and closed my eyes. I wanted to capture and savor the moment. As the mental picture of my departure slowly faded, I began to meditate on God's Word. All of a sudden, I was stricken by two horrible thoughts that caused me to jump up in my seat. "Would this be another hopeless failure? Would I return to my old way of life?" Memories and visions of the past tormented my mind. I had to be careful not to entertain such thoughts because I didn't want to act upon them. The Scriptures reveal that *"every man is tempted, when he is drawn away of his own lust, and enticed. Then when lust hath conceived, it bringeth forth sin: and sin, when it is finished, bringeth forth death."* In the past, this demonic cycle predicted and projected failure to my future. The devil used the strategy of evil remembrance to bombard my mind into sin. Later, I found out that a demon called "memory recall" was the culprit. When the enemy came in like a flood, the Spirit of God lifted up a standard against him.

I meditated on the Scripture that people in Christ are new creatures. Although I was familiar with this verse, I really didn't understand it. I knew something divine and dynamic had happened because I thought, felt, spoke, and acted differently. At that stage of my spiritual walk, to actually believe that I was a new person was too much for me to swallow and digest. I had a lot to learn.

The trip began. During the hours that passed, I yielded myself to the Trinity. As I sought the Lord in prayer, I earnestly requested His supernatural help to never be a failure again. I told God that I wanted my life to count for something good for a change. As a newborn believer, it didn't take long for me to realize that I was totally dependent upon God for everything. I recalled the countless instances in the past when I desired self-change and attempted individual betterment through my own power. At such times, I failed miserably. Those attempts were just that. Attempts. They didn't avail me anything but frustration, pain, and heartache. The bottom line was if God didn't change me, I wasn't going to change.

Deep down in my heart I desperately desired great change. I wanted change more than anything. I was sick and tired of hurting myself and other people. Because of my spiritual transformation, I no longer enjoyed using or abusing others. Christ's selflessness destroyed my selfishness.

The mere thought of the change to come brought tears to my eyes. Yet a deeper cry existed within me. It was the cry of unceasing passion and unadulterated hunger for more of God. I wanted to known intimately the Jesus described and detailed in the four Gospels. And I didn't want to wait any longer. I wanted this firsthand revelation NOW! In my heart and mind, I had waited long enough. I needed to know why Jesus saved me and what purpose He had for my life.

As I meditated upon the meaning of my salvation, the Holy Ghost spoke to me and exposed the previous lie of the devil. He reassured me that my life was going to be completely different. I believed God's Witness of truth and wept with a heavenly joy that I never experienced before. This particular bus trip was much more enjoyable than any of my previous trips.

Newness of Life

13

I STARED OUT THE BUS WINDOW THROUGH RED, TEAR-stained eyes. From the distance of the road, the scenery appeared tranquil and refreshing. I again took great pleasure in the small things of life. The first thing I noticed was that the trees stood very straight. Just then, the gift of revelation began to operate. They were perpendicular to the earth and pointed up, straight toward heaven. Trees are a key part of creation. God utilized one tree—the tree of life—to transfer the life of heaven to the entire earth. In addition, man was created from the living dust of the ground. Trees play another vital part in man's existence. They absorb carbon dioxide, convert it chemically, and emit oxygen. This oxygen supplies life to every creature that moves upon the face of the earth—including man and woman.

As I sized up the trees, I followed my gaze upward and intersected a series of clouds. I couldn't esteem trees properly without revering the clouds that filled the sky. Clouds are a type of aerial sponge that absorb the evaporated water of the earth and dispense it again at an appointed time. This process occurs over and over in a cycle of replenishment. Water as falling rain is essential to all manner of life.

I experienced a newness of life that is not found in anything or anyone other than Jesus Christ. Inspiration flowed and revelation occurred like never before. For the first time in my life, I observed the abundant wonderful works of God that are on display everywhere. Nature is God's handiwork. It displays His hand at work. The earth and all of its life point to God's greatest creation—

mankind. Humanity was originally given dominion over all of the creatures of the earth. Adam relinquished God's omniauthority to Satan through sin. But Jesus returned all authority to the Church through His death, resurrection, and glorification.

The realization that man was made in the image of God brought me great comfort. But the reality that I now knew the Creator of the universe blew me away. The interpersonal relationship I had with God gave me a sense of belonging that I never had before. I finally felt important, accepted, and realized that God really cared. I also experienced perfect love for the first time. I identified with David when he pondered God's interest in man. The Psalmist asked the Supreme Being, "*What is man, that thou art mindful of him? and the son of man, that thou visitest him?*" Man was created below the angels, yet God exalted humankind above them. I was happy that God cared enough to watch over me when no one else regarded me, my livelihood, or my future.

As I meditated upon that thought, the Holy Spirit revealed something to me about my past. The day that I overdosed in the crack house, I could and should have died. Death was literally knocking at my heart. The only reason my heart didn't explode was because God was mindful of me. At that time, He extended His mercy and winked at my foolish ways. I am forever grateful that God loved, spared, and saved me.

I fell asleep after several hours of revelation and eight hours of grueling travel. I rested in the comfort of knowing God, being special to Him, and being a vital part of the Body of Christ. God gave me self-worth and many reasons to live and do right. I slept all night until 6:00 a.m.

I was abruptly awakened by the sudden stop of the bus. As I wiped the night from my eyes, I was directly confronted with two golden arches. I hoped it was the reflection of the morning sun on the St. Louis Arch, but that was wishful thinking. Unfortunately, it was the local McDonald's. I was extremely disappointed. Apparently, the bus hadn't traveled as far as I thought and temporarily stopped for gas and group breakfast. I was very hungry but only had the $20 my mother gave me.

There were many hours ahead, and I had to ration my money wisely. The trip was a minimum of 34 hours to my final destination.

I pulled myself from my slumbered position, forced my legs to work, got to my feet, and staggered off the bus. After receiving my food, the first thing I did was check my spiritual walk. I needed to know that my newfound spiritual Friend was still with me and in me. As I closed my eyes to bless my food, I felt the overwhelming presence of the Lord. The Holy Spirit reminded me of Matthew 28:20 when Jesus said, *"I am with you alway, even unto the end of the world."* This meant Jesus Christ would never leave me or forsake me. Everywhere I went, He went also. And everything I endured, He bore with me. The indwelling of His person by the Holy Ghost was permanent—never to change. Glory! What a wonderful promise and fulfilling experience. God was more real than I had ever thought or imagined.

About 30 minutes later, the driver motioned for all passengers to return to the bus. Like a group of anxious travelers, we responded appropriately and quickly reboarded. Obviously, everyone had a greater destination than McDonald's. Off we went. On the road again. The bus resumed its speed and traveled at an unrelenting pace. It too seemed destined.

I was in for a big surprise as we neared the state of Kentucky. To my amazement, I looked out the window and saw the great Rocky Mountains. This was the first time I ever saw mountains. They were incredibly immense in size and permanently anchored in place. You talk about a firm foundation...this was it! These peaks weren't going anywhere. Everywhere I looked and everything I saw reminded me of a Scripture. The great Rocky Mountains reminded me of Jesus the Rock, the Chief Cornerstone of the Church. Another verse came to mind. The commonly quoted but little practiced Matthew 17:20, which states, *"If ye have faith as a grain of mustard seed, ye shall say unto this mountain, Remove hence to yonder place; and it shall remove; and nothing shall be impossible unto you."*

I envisioned myself commanding the Rockies to be removed from their current location and cast into the sea. I wondered why Jesus used a mountain in this parable. Then the reason hit me. In a literal sense, it is impossible for man to move a mountain with his natural ability. It is too big, heavy, and massive. But nothing is too difficult for the Maker of the mountain. In a figurative sense, some situations in life are impossible for man to resolve with his own strength. At such times, he needs the hand of the Lord and the assistance of His omnipotent Spirit. This indicates even mountainous circumstances that appear immovable will be removed when God's-kind of faith is present and divine inspiration is decreed. All things are possible to those who believe in God's almighty ability.

I checked my watch. It was 8:00 a.m. on the nose. My mind momentarily traveled back in time to my prison days. I wondered what my one-time fellow inmates were doing. Then it dawned on me that they were starting their daily work detail. Some were assigned to work inside the fence, others on the outside of the fence. Either way, prison work was a losing battle. It consisted of hard labor and no pay with no chance of escape. It was the same thing day after day, week after week, month after month, and year after year. I thanked God that He delivered me from that life of bondage.

Although I was permanently freed from that system, I had compassion on those who were still imprisoned. This was most uncharacteristic of me, but very characteristic of Jesus. The Holy Ghost gave me a spiritual burden for those who were yet in prison. It was not like me to think and care about others in such a pure way. This new mind-set was due to God in my life. His unconditional love stirred within me to such an extent that I actually prayed for my confined friends from the past. It didn't seem fair that I was free and they remained in bondage. Also, it didn't seem right not to do something about it. After all, Frank, Robert, Herbert, Max, Phil, and countless others were still subject to Satan's grip of sin and captivity. It was through this experience that God opened my eyes to one of His calls upon my life—to the outcast, downcast, and castaways.

TC: The Place for Me

14

THE BUS PLUGGED ALONG ON ITS SEEMINGLY ENDLESS journey. Man and machine co-labored to arrive at the appointed destination. After 34-1/2 hours of exhaustive travel, Muskegon, Michigan, was spotted on the horizon. Adrenaline and nervous energy shot throughout my body. My heart pounded in anticipation of getting on with my life.

We entered the city limits, drove down the main road, and came to the entrance of the station. As the bus pulled into the terminal, I beheld a blue van to my right with the words "Teen Challenge" painted on it. I breathed a great sigh of relief. Deliverance was in sight, gassed up, and waiting to take me to the Promised Land. When I saw that the group from Teen Challenge had already arrived, a wave of fulfillment drenched me. After my grueling bus ride, the last thing I wanted to do was wait several more hours at an unfamiliar bus stop in the middle of nowhere.

The coach came to an abrupt, final halt. I jumped up from my seat, retrieved my overnight duffel bag from the overhead compartment, and slung it over my shoulder. I quickly exited the bus expecting to greet someone, enter the van, and be on my merry way. It was not to be. I approached the van and noticed that nobody was inside. I concluded that the driver was inside the depot. I moseyed over to the bus station but didn't see any representatives from Teen Challenge. The only people in sight were a station clerk and a beautiful young lady who appeared to be a fashion model.

I thought to myself, "Surely, she can't be from Teen Challenge.

The driver must be in the bathroom or something."

Just to make sure, I walked over to the young woman and said, "Excuse me, do you know where the people are who own that van?"

To my surprise and delight, she responded, "Yes! I'm the person driving that van!"

Formal introductions were in order.

"Hello, my name is Shawn Mosley." As soon as I mentioned my name, the model lit up like a Christmas tree.

"You're Shawn Mosley?" she asked.

Her response took me totally off guard. I returned her question with an equally emphatic response.

"Yes, I am!"

To my amazement, she backed up a few feet and looked me over a couple of times as if she knew me or something. I was a little embarrassed and it showed on my face.

"Brother...I love you!"

I was so shocked that I responded without even thinking.

"I love you too!"

Truly, it was love at first sight. From that moment on, our love was settled. We were destined for each other before the foundation of the world.

My first impression of Teen Challenge was a great one! What a tremendous experience. I hoped all future introductions were like my first. I got off to a very good start. The first thought that entered my mind was, "I wonder if this is how they greet all of the new prospects?" That thought was followed by doubt and skepticism, "I wonder if this is some kind of setup?"

The beautiful woman who loved me explained why she was so excited to meet Shawn Mosley. She introduced herself as Marie Dail. Then she informed me that she and my sister Melissa were very good friends. Marie related that the two of them had been interceding for me for the past six months. I was overjoyed to hear and know that someone loved me enough to pray for me.

After the nervous jitters and small talk ceased, I looked at Marie and said, "I don't see any reason to prolong the trip. Shall we go?"

The truth of the matter was I was willing to go anywhere with Miss Dail. She spoiled the moment and situation by informing me of the gender rules at Teen Challenge. Men and women were not allowed to communicate with each other unless he or she was an authorized staff member. I couldn't believe it. As she continued, it got worse. Women were strictly forbidden to escort men by themselves. Female staff could only transport female students. Male staff could only transport male students. Reality settled in and two horrors struck me. First, Marie and I were forced to part ways. Second, I was stuck at the bus terminal for another two hours after all. I was very disappointed.

Marie broke the silence and said, "I'll call the men's center and tell them that you're here. Someone will come by and pick you up shortly."

Even though I was weary from waiting I said, "Okay." I wasn't about to argue with Marie. After all, she loved me. It was the love of God that drew and bonded me with Teen Challenge.

Marie made the telephone call and returned. Contact was made and a staff member was on his way. Then she climbed into the van, slammed the door, started the engine, slammed it in drive, and rushed down the road. She left without saying a word to me. As she sped away, I wondered if I would ever see her again. Evidently, the young woman Marie came to pick up experienced an unexpected delay in her trip.

After an hour or two of loitering at the bus terminal, my ride finally arrived. A Brother by the name of Tyrone drove the van. He apologized for the delay and explained that he had to pick up some students from the Laundromat because it was laundry day.

Tyrone was tall, dark-skinned, and physically well-groomed. In time, I discovered he was just as sharp spiritually as he was naturally. But as sharp as Tyrone was, he was no substitute for Marie Doll...I mean Marie Dail. No one was. She was one in five billion. When God made Marie, He broke the mold.

Tyrone opened up to me immediately. He was originally from Tampa, Florida, and had graduated from the program with honors. For the last five years, he was a member of the staff. Tyrone gave me the lowdown on procedures and protocol. It required the subjection of the flesh and all carnal desires. The first truth he related was that it took a tremendous amount of discipline and self-control to graduate from Teen Challenge. To pass with honors, no exceptions could be made. For example, men couldn't look at women students. If a man did and was caught, he was reprimanded by missing a meal. Also, men students couldn't talk in line. If this rule was violated, the penalty was a missed meal for the first offense and an all day work detail for each subsequent offense. Tyrone went on and on and on with the rules. I thought he would never stop. I felt as if I were back in prison! To me, all of these rules sounded like legalism. I asked myself, "What in the world have I gotten myself into?"

Tyrone and I drove for another 20 minutes until we arrived at the final destination. Like it or not, 440 Pontaluna Road was my home for the next 13 months. So I better get used to it.

Again, more introductions were in order. During such times I kept my front up and discerned the other person until I figured him out. The first Brother I met was Beotis Clark from Atlanta, Georgia. I admired him because he had great love and a strong devotion to God. Beotis had a charismatic, infectious personality that broke the ice in tense situations. The first thing he said to me was "What's up, home boy?"

His genuine smile displayed the joy of the Lord that was inside. Beotis greeted me with a supernatural warmth that made me feel right at home. From the moment of our introduction, he became a good Christian role model in my life. When the other students played sports or goofed off during the scheduled free time, Beotis removed himself from these carnal activities. He remained inside the dormitory, praying to God and studying his Bible. I respected the seriousness of his commitment and conviction. His desire to fulfill God's call upon his life was a continual inspiration to me.

Beotis checked my luggage and me in. Some parts of life never change. Like Marie Dail, he was also very happy to see me. I found out that his fianceé and my sister were also good friends. In fact, word of my arrival in Muskegon was anticipated across the campus. Rumor had it that Melissa was so excited about my enrollment at

Teen Challenge that she ran through her dormitory screaming as if she had just won a million dollars.

The overall atmosphere at Teen Challenge was positive, peaceful, and pleasant. The presence of God was so pervasive that I discerned it as soon as I entered the main facility. As I stood in the lobby, I realized this place housed over 200 X-cons and X-drug addicts. Despite their cumulative evil pasts, an unexplainable peace filled the atmosphere. It was overwhelming and refreshing at the same time. At that moment, I was sure of two things. First, Teen Challenge was the place for me. Second, it was exactly where I was supposed to be.

The First Chapel Service

15

THE NEXT DAY, I WENT TO MY FIRST IN-HOUSE SERVICE. As soon as I set foot inside the chapel, I encountered the glory of the Lord. The presence of God was so thick and intense that it made me tremble. Literally. The biblical truth of Luke 7:47—"those who are forgiven of much, love much"—was in full manifestation around me. I marveled at the unification of the male and female voices in attendance. They praised God with great passion and intimacy. Exalted worship came from their restored hearts and renewed spirits. Every word in every song meant everything to them. It was obvious how thankful they were. God was all I needed. I was hooked on Jesus for life and forever.

The chapel services at Teen Challenge are unique and unforgettable. They are glorious to say the least. Everyone should experience at least one in his or her lifetime.

I felt comfortable and at ease in the services. At that same time, I had butterflies in my stomach. One of the reasons I was nervous was because I wasn't used to the glory of God. The other reason was that I was in the same building as my sister Melissa for the first time in a long time. Melissa was sitting on the left side with the women. I was sitting on the right side with the men. Despite our close proximity and desire for reunion, we were absolutely forbidden to communicate with each other especially during chapel. Service time was when men and women concentrated and gave their all to God.

Although it was against the rules and I knew better, I tried to sneak a peak at Melissa out of the corner of my eye. Instead of catching a glimpse of sis', I spotted Brother Tyrone ready to bust anyone looking around. Family or not, I wasn't about to get caught. I liked to eat and couldn't afford to miss a meal. Although I was only 165 pounds, I had the appetite of an elephant. Melissa would have to wait.

A few minutes later, an unknown man entered the chapel through the side door. He was on the short side, approximately five feet two inches tall. I immediately discerned him as a father in the Spirit. Although small in bodily stature, he appeared to be a giant in the things of God. My curiosity eventually got the best of me. I had to know the identity of this man.

I leaned over and asked the person sitting next to me, "Who's that?"

"Brother McClain…the director," he whispered.

My first impression was a lasting one. There was an authoritative firmness about Brother McClain. It was obvious from his appearance that no one messed with this man of God. He took the things of God very seriously—as all ministers should. When it came to the Bible, he was strictly business. God's business, that is! This was evident when he stepped up to the pulpit. He stood at that platform hour after hour and imparted the Word of God. His intense preaching brought conviction to every soul in attendance. Every person within the sound of his voice was brought to a place of self-evaluation.

Many of the chapel services Brother McClain conducted ended in weeping and genuine repentance. In contrast to his spiritual fervency, he was also a man of great love and compassion. He was serious yet sweet. He knew when to be tough and when to be gentle. It was common knowledge that Brother McClain spent many hours before God interceding and travailing for the well-being of his students. During this time he received the grace to minister righteously. This son of King Jesus became my first spiritual father. I regarded him as such for the remainder of my stay at Teen Challenge.

After my first chapel service, I was called to the front to be reunited with my closest sister. I was elated to finally see, hear, feel, and speak with my own flesh and blood. In the past I thought I would never see her again. Thank God I was wrong!

Melissa and I made eye contact and embraced each other. We

sobbed bitterly in the presence of the Lord before the entire congregation of students. Afterward, many of our Brothers and Sisters in Christ came forward and ministered to us. As middle children, we were both rejected by man. But now, we were both accepted in the beloved by God. The black sheep were now whole and adopted into the family of heaven on earth.

At Teen Challenge, I learned the true meaning of brotherly love. Over two hundred men and women who were in bondage to alcohol, drugs, and other vices were taught how to reach out to the hurting and needy with God's love flowing through their hearts. We also learned the true meaning of Christian discipleship. First and foremost, a disciple was a disciplined person who obeyed the written and spoken Word as well as the leading of the Holy Spirit. True disciples say "Yes" to God and "No" to Satan.

When a person first becomes born again, he or she is still dominated by the sin nature that exists within the unrenewed mind and unsubmitted body. At Teen Challenge we learned to submit our bodies unto God as a living sacrifice that was pure, holy, and acceptable to our Maker. It was also explained that our battle was spiritual, not natural. Believers do not wrestle against flesh and blood but against demonic principalities, evil powers, the dark rulers of this world, wicked spirits in the heavens, and demons in sinners and saints alike. In addition, we were instructed how to pull down the demonic spirits who influenced our minds, to cast down evil imaginations, and everything that exalted itself against the Lordship of Jesus Christ. In essence, we learned how to subdue every thought to the doctrines and principles of the Bible. To be victorious, God had to be obeyed at all times.

One of the biggest problems most new converts have is in their sexual character. For most people, their fleshly desires have run wild for years. Here's what normally happens. A person who has lived in sexual sin for two or three decades will get saved. Because of spiritual ignorance, he or she won't know what to do with his or her body. Just because a person accepts Christ does not automatically nullify the desires or cravings within. I am referring to the sexual appetite and

God's command to be fruitful and multiply. To overcome this curse and bondage, the students at Teen Challenge are enrolled in a four session class called "Victory over Sin, Satan, and Evil Thoughts." These classes teach one and all how to combat the wiles of the devil with the written Word of God. In addition, students are encouraged to regularly submit themselves for deliverance. Many evil desires are removed when demons are cast out of the body and soul.

I can honestly say that I loved *every* minute of my stay at Teen Challenge. While the other guys spent their free time playing baseball or participating in some other sporting event, I followed in the footsteps of Beotis Clark and Brother McClain. I knew that the path to everlasting life was very narrow. Therefore, I stayed in my dorm room and read the Bible or prayed. When Jesus made His royal entrance into my life, my conversion was genuine and deep-rooted. This is why I could never get enough of God. Private time was absolutely essential. As a result of my daily fellowship, God became as real to me as my hand.

Because of His great mercy toward me, I vowed to never leave or forsake God no matter how difficult things got. Luke 9:62 alludes to this for he who sets his hand to the plow and regretfully looks back to his past is not fit for the Kingdom of Heaven.

Time flew quickly. Before I knew it, my day to graduate from Teen Challenge was approaching. Consequently, I had to prepare for the challenges that faced me in the real world. This time, however, I wasn't worried or afraid. Two truths grounded and rooted me. First, God was with me. Second, He was forever in me. My heart, mind, and body were prepared to serve Him all the days of my life—at all costs.

I grabbed hold to the things of God quickly. To achieve spiritual growth I required fellowship, and fellowship required prayer. But I had two big problems. First, I didn't know how to pray. Second, I never formally prayed before. In the past, God honored my attempts and winked at my crude methods. The time had come to communicate with God His way through prayer. Therefore, I was forced to study the Bible like never before. During this period, the Holy Spirit revealed the secrets of earnest petition. It wasn't long before I saw my heartfelt prayers answered and fulfilled. I realized that God and prayer were my hopes to continual life and long-term success. Jesus was my Savior and I trusted God to answer all of my prayers according to His will for my life.

One day a fellow student gave me a cassette tape from a minister by the name of E. V. Hill. The message on this tape was called "Trust Me." I listened to the sermon with great expectation, for I always looked forward to spiritual growth. After a few minutes, God's servant began to preach like a wild man. His message brought tears to my eyes and heaven to earth. My dorm room was actually filled with the presence of God.

Halfway into the sermon, I realized it was recorded at his wife's funeral. His message revealed that of all the people on the earth, Christians face the most difficult trials and tribulations. When they come, believers must trust God more than ever. They must realize that God does not lie or repent. God will not allow His children to be tested beyond what they can bear. Rather, God will make a way for that person to escape the temptation. God used this minister to establish a foundation of maturity in my life. To this day, I reflect on that message and the truths Dr. E. V. Hill imparted whenever I encounter spiritual and natural adversity.

At periodic times throughout my stay, I realized how vital this time was in my life. I knew beyond a shadow of a doubt that God singled me out from the billions of people on earth and strategically placed me at Teen Challenge. During the year, I repeatedly examined myself, identified my shortcomings, and appropriated God's Word as the solution. It worked and I changed. But the change was too slow. So I worked on my faults with a vengeance. I looked within and saw a wretch undone with many problems. I cried out to my Savior from the depths of my spirit and pleaded for personal renewal. He heard my plea, answered accordingly, and changed me. I hid no aspect of my three-part being from God. How could I? After all, He lived in me and knew everything about me.

I worshiped God in spirit and in truth. I concentrated on the truth part. Most people approach God and explain how good they are in exchange for His blessings. But it was just the opposite for me. I approached God as I was—a new creature defiled by past sin and habits who desperately desired permanent transformation. More than anything, I wanted to be a godly man. I earnestly desired to be known, respected, and received as a man of God. Such a task required great change. No problem! I was willing and God was able. As a direct result of my honesty, the Holy Ghost showed me my true spiritual identity. As He did, I received the revelation of who I really was in Christ. When I realized how the Trinity actually perceived me, my life was revolutionized.

The Transformation of the Mind

16

MY FAVORITE TIME OF THE DAY AT TEEN Challenge was evening prayer, which began promptly at 6:30. All of the men gathered in the chapel and prayed until heaven visited. In my estimation, there's nothing more glorious than one hundred men united under one roof with one purpose—to seek and be with God. Through this experience, I again beheld the manifestation of Luke 7:47, those who are forgiven of much, love much. All persons in attendance—be they small or big, young or old, black or white—expressed their thanks for forgiveness and salvation.

During my first evening prayer session, I sought an altar of privacy. I found my refuge in a corner under an old, maneuverable pulpit. Every night at 6:30, I entered my personal sanctuary and cried out to my Heavenly Father until I felt His person. This altar became my hiding place, my place of refuge, and my place of communion. The presence of the Lord became my new home. Sometimes, the Holy Spirit came upon me so strongly until I couldn't stand it anymore. God's person was so real and thick that I had to leave the chapel. Other times, I surrendered, was filled with God's new wine, and experienced drunkenness in the Spirit. The Bible confirms this in Ephesians 5:18, for it is written, *"Be not drunk with wine, wherein is excess, but be filled with the Spirit...."* Sometimes, the baptism was so heavy that I actually forgot how to talk and walk.

During these fervent prayer sessions, I saw several divine visions of God's hand washing my mind with the blood of Jesus. Oh, how my heart longed for more of my Lord! Soon thereafter, the Holy Spirit dealt with me concerning the words of my mouth. I had to watch my words because my tongue was a world of iniquity. The Holy Ghost revealed that my tongue was a powerful life force. Life and death as words actually proceeded out of my mouth. Over the years, it had spewed enough death. Now it was time to minister life. I surrendered my voice and words to God because I didn't want to offend the precious Holy Spirit, whom I loved and appreciated so much.

Although Teen Challenge is a place where God's Word is continually preached and taught, not everyone was as serious about God as I was. I wanted God in all aspects of my life—all the way. If I found myself intermingling with a lukewarm Christian, I quickly cut him off. As I maintained this attitude, I despised the things of my past such as swearing, lying, violence, and fornication. The Scripture "*Abstain from all appearance of evil*" was adopted as my new way of life. This verse became a reality to me because the first thing God does with His covenant people is show them who they are in His glory.

The Bible informs humanity that none are righteous and man's good deeds are as filthy rags unto the Lord. However, by accepting Jesus Christ and His work at Calvary, believers are cleansed by His blood and clothed with His robe of righteousness. Born again Christians are righteous only because of the cross, death, burial, resurrection, glorification, and eternal life of Jesus Christ. No matter how much a person matures in his or her walk with God, there is always room for more improvement. Daily I thanked God that He showed me my faults so I could pray and choose them away.

Many of the Brothers at Teen Challenge came to me privately and confessed their secret faults. They did this because they knew I walked in grace and mercy and wouldn't condemn them. At such times, the stronger needed to help the weaker. I encouraged them to change their ways. Then I ministered to them in the spirit of restoration as the Holy Ghost directed me. Concerning restoration, the Bible declares that God will restore the years "*that the locust hath eaten, the cankerworm, and the caterpillar, and the palmerworm....*" This Scripture encompasses all aspects of human life—be it past, present, and future. In the process, God replaces the mind-set of sin with the mind of Christ. When given the occasion, God always restores a new believer and never condemns him or her. Therefore, I did as God would have done. I instructed my Brothers in the Lord to arise from their spiritual stupor, shake off the heavy bands of sin, and keep trying until they had the victory. God believes in truth and success, not error and loss.

At Teen Challenge we learned how to bring out the best in each other. Everyone was in the same spiritual boat. We were cut, bleeding, dying, and in dire need of the Great Physician to perform life and death surgery. No one dared pull the plug of the respirator that sustained a young believer. After all, no one was fully functional. God's Respirator, who is the Holy Ghost, pumped the essential spiritual oxygen into the spirit, soul, and body of every X-drug addict, prostitute, gang banger, and outcast.

One day during my work duties, a Brother from Chicago named Maurice walked into my room. He explained how difficult it was for him to walk uprightly before the Lord. Apparently, he was an X-pimp who used to shoot heroin every day. Maurice tried to convince me that he wasn't cut out to be a Christian. The truth of the matter was he bought a lie and had begun to compromise. Maurice was looking for someone who would accept and approve his excuse so he could revert to his old ways. When Maurice explained the situation with his mouth, I discerned his heart. His spirit was willing, but his unrenewed mind was adverse to God's will, and demons in his flesh craved the drug. At that infant stage in his walk, Maurice didn't need me to be hard on him. He desperately needed the Word of Truth and a word of encouragement. God inspired and supplied both. I gave him Scriptures and told him to bury the past and resurrect his future in Christ.

1 Peter 4:12-13 says, *"Beloved, think it not strange concerning the fiery trial which is to try you...But rejoice, inasmuch as ye are partakers of Christ's sufferings...."* As the unified Body of the Lord, the Church needs to expose the common problems of sin and bondage, and deal with them according to the Bible. This is necessary to inform new converts who feel they are the only ones with problems. Think it not

strange. You're not alone. The Church must allow those who have overcome these temptations to be visible witnesses that victory is possible. God is no respecter of persons. What God does for one, He will do for another. If God brought another believer out of a life of sin and bondage, He will deliver you too! For saints overcome the devil *"by the blood of the Lamb, and by the word of their testimony...."*

Recognizing the Call

17

AT TEEN CHALLENGE, EVERY NIGHT EXCLUDING weekends, we had a two hour study session from 7:00 p.m. to 9:00 p.m. During this time we fervently studied the Word of God. We memorized Scriptures and emphasized each book in the Bible. This continued day after day, week after week, and month after month. After many sessions, I thought I had the Bible down to a science. How wrong I was. In 2 Corinthians 3:6 the Bible says, *"the letter killeth...."* Knowing the law of God's Word is both good and bad. It can cause a new convert to get puffed up with pride, which can be detrimental, destructive, and devastating. As far as I'm concerned, there are too many novices in fivefold ministry and the Body of Christ. Amen? Amen!

I want to emphasize the second half of the verse above. It is written that the letter or law killeth. But it is also written that the Spirit giveth life. In other words, the Holy Ghost gives life to the Word of God. He does this by breathing upon the *Logos* Word, which transforms it into living *Rhema*. Jesus confirmed this, for He revealed that the Word without the Spirit is unproductive and unprofitable. Many theologians and seminarians have a head knowledge of the Bible. Yet these same ministers distort and disbelieve many realities of the Gospel. It takes the Holy Ghost to give them heart revelation of a principle or passage. Otherwise, the life of that Scripture is not communicated and imparted to that person. At such times the Bible is reduced to ink and dead words on paper.

The Spirit of God takes the events that happened two thousand years ago and makes them real. He also takes the trials and tribulations of the first century Church and relates them to your current predicament. When asked, the Holy Ghost will introduce the right solutions for your everyday problems, needs, and desires.

As I studied the Word of God, the Holy Ghost began to open up my understanding of the Scriptures. This is similar to what Jesus did with the 12 disciples, which is documented in Luke 24:45. For example, take the situation of the Samaritan woman recorded in John 4. The problem wasn't that she had five previous husbands and a live-in mate. The real issue was living water. She was thirsty for love and life. As so many do, the woman attempted to solve a spiritual problem with natural solutions. She tried to quench her thirst for love by getting involved in different marital relationships. The woman at the well never received love at some point in her past. When she didn't find or receive it from her first husband, she moved on to another, then another, then another, then another, then another. That same instant, I saw the light of this passage in relation to my past. I too was thirsty for love. I never received it at home. I tried to find it in all the wrong places doing all the wrong things. My desire for acceptance, love, and purpose was found in "The Thirst Quencher." Today and forever, Jesus Christ is the *only* solution!

Through this single passage, God showed me the root problem of cons, pushers, pimps, prostitutes, gang bangers, and other deviants. All of these people are trying to quench their insatiable thirst through alcohol, drugs, sex, money, and violence. In the process, they rebel against the norm, society, and God. Their destructive actions really indicate that they long for a personal relationship with God through Jesus Christ.

During my last days at Teen Challenge, God began to give me visions, dreams, and desires for the outcasts of society. Specifically, inner city gangs and those locked away in prisons. Many times during a vision, my heart and spirit cried out to God on behalf of these captives. It was then that I began to get a clearer picture of my call and ministry. I remember one vision in particular. I saw multitudes of the most gruesome, hardened criminals coming to Christ, flooding church altars everywhere, and repenting for their wickedness. They were desperate for the life-transforming power of Jesus Christ!

Saint or sinner, know this. No matter who you are or how strong you are—every man, woman, and child has a **BREAKING POINT**. This is the moment that your self-control and will collapses under trial. It is the point an individual reaches when his or her endurance gives way. When you come to your **BREAKING POINT**, if you call on Jesus, He will pick up the shattered pieces and put you back together. For whosoever calls upon the name of the Lord shall be saved, healed, and delivered.

On May 9, 1992, I graduated from Teen Challenge at the top of my class. Also, do you remember that beautiful model I met at the Muskegon bus terminal by the name of Marie Dail? Well...I finally got up the nerve and proposed. To my absolute delight, she accepted and we were married shortly thereafter. Marie not only became my wife, but also the mother of my first child. Together, as husband and wife, we are serving the Lord. We have accepted and entered into God's call for our lives and minister as needed throughout the nation. Truly, old things have passed away and all things are new. With God, *nothing* is impossible!

My Decision for Christ

In Isaiah 61:1 it is written, "*The Spirit of the Lord God is upon me; because the Lord hath anointed me to preach good tidings unto the meek; he hath sent me to bind up the brokenhearted, to proclaim liberty to the captives, and the opening of the prison to them that are bound....*" This verse was fulfilled two thousand years ago by Jesus of Nazareth. Luke 4:18 confirms that Christ was anointed by the Holy Ghost to declare the Gospel to the poor, to heal those at their **BREAKING POINT**, to minister deliverance to the convicts, and to free the imprisoned.

Everything I shared in this book is true. Please don't make the same mistakes that I did. You still have time to get right with God. Do it now...before it's too late. Today is your day of salvation! At this time I would like to invite you to make Jesus Christ the Lord of your life. If you confess with your mouth that "Jesus is Lord," and believe in your heart that God raised Him from the dead, you will be saved. For with the heart man believes unto righteousness, and with the mouth confession is made unto salvation. To receive Jesus Christ as your personal Lord and Savior, repeat this prayer from your heart:

Jesus, I believe that You died for me at Calvary and rose from the dead three days later. I confess that I am a sinner who needs Your love, mercy, and forgiveness. Come into my heart right now. Grant me salvation and eternal life. From this moment forward, I will love You and live for You all the days of my life. Thank You. Amen.

Signed Date

My wife and I want to hear from you. Please take a minute to sign this form and mail this page to the address below. We will respond accordingly.

Shawn and Marie Mosley
Breaking Point Ministries
P. O. Box 4436
Muskegon Heights, MI 49444

SPIRITUAL BIOGRAPHY

Shawn Mosley is a young man called to reach the inner city youth for God. He is a dynamic speaker who touches and transforms the downcast, outcast, and castaways. The Holy Spirit has anointed this man of God as a weapon of change to minister healing and deliverance to the captives.

THE BREAKING POINT is liberating countless people who are in bondage to Satan and his evil deceptions. Because saints overcome the devil by the word of their testimony, this book is guaranteed by heaven to set the bound free! It is opening prison doors—spiritually, soulishly, and naturally—around the world!

If you have enjoyed this book and would like to order additional copies of **THE BREAKING POINT**, send $9.95 plus $2.00 shipping and handling to:

Breaking Point Ministries
P. O. Box 4436
Muskegon Heights, MI 49444

If you have been blessed by this testimony and are interested in contacting Shawn and Marie Mosley, please write to them at the above address. Thank you.